Wild Wise Women

Compiled by
SANDRA STACHOWICZ

Grab Your Free Gifts Now!

Access incredible bonuses worth £2,997

Just to say thank you for trusting us, we would like to grant you instant access to incredible bonuses worth £2,997, including some of the best tools, techniques, and video training so you can **exponentially transform your self-worth, body, business, relationships, energy, and finances**.

These bonuses will help you create extraordinary results in your business and life, unlocking the keys to creating your best year yet.

Click here to get started: http://wildwisewomen.club/

Dedication

I dedicate this compilation to my mother Dorota, a wild wise woman, and to ALL the mothers in the world.

Little Wild Wise Woman

"Wild women are an unexplainable spark of life. They ooze freedom and seek awareness, they belong to nobody but themselves yet give a piece of who they are to everyone they meet.

If you have met one, hold on to her, she'll allow you into her chaos but she'll also show you her magic."

— Nikki Rowe

Acknowledgments

I would like to thank all the authors for their inspiring contributions, for meeting deadlines, and for their unwavering enthusiasm and support throughout. This book is a showcase of their genius and reflects all the hard they put into making this book possible.

Special thanks to Andrea McCurry for her patience and unparalleled dedication to this project, making sense of all the chaos, her invaluable rainbow-coloured suggestions (we shall cherish them forever), and for expertly editing everyone's stories.

Table of Contents

Introduction

"Every woman has a story. Every woman has power. The power is in her story." — Tobi Schwartz-Cassell

On the surface it may look like you have it all together. The perfect partner, the perfect mother, the perfect entrepreneur. Yet, behind the scenes of the everyday mundane the ugly truth is revealed…

This book is about anything BUT perfect.

If you're looking for a recipe to have the perfect body, the perfect relationship, or the perfect life you won't find any here. *Wild Wise Women* depicts real stories from real women and women's lives are anything but perfect. This book contains truth-tales from perfectly imperfect yet fearless women entrepreneurs because that is what essentially makes them real.

Once you lift the lid of the façade and peek into her heart, you'll discover that no woman is immune to failures, weaknesses, or disappointments. Yet, amongst her less-than-perfect replicas, there's one woman that stands out and it's not because she is perfect, in fact, far from it.

She's one of a kind simply because she is not afraid of making mistakes. The wild woman never makes the same mistake twice. Undeterred, she continually adds onto her repertoire and makes a new, better one. In fact, making mistakes is what makes her strong and beautiful.

The wild and wise woman displays her shortcomings proudly, carrying them around as if they were a baby, drawing in from her inner wisdom, the innate wisdom of her womb. The wisdom holder knows her failures are lessons in disguise and she's more than keen to play peek-a-boo to draw strength from them and to embrace them.

Wild women are enigmatic creatures. They are an inexplicable force of nature and one that should be reckoned with. A wild woman guards her secrets as if her life depended on them until she knows it's time to open her Pandora's box and let "strictly-classified information" spill over.

This is what this book is about, real stories from real women.

Every woman has a story, one full of secrets, moral lessons, and just as many disappointments. The more painful and challenging the entrepreneurial journey, the more powerful the learnings.

The wild woman knows that her stories, no matter how personal or painful, are not hers to keep and she shares her wisdom willingly and abundantly, safe in the knowing that her truth-tales have the power to heal and transform the world, one story, one woman, one business at a time.

In *Wild Wise Women: 10 Stories of Fearless Females Relentless in Pursuit of Their Dreams, Success and Happiness,* real women from all walks of life share their unique and sometimes, harrowing entrepreneurial journeys, full of unwavering hope, inner strength, and resilience.

Wild Wise Women is the quest of 10 fearless women entrepreneurs who beat all the odds and survived the unimaginable in order to become successful.

This book reveals:

- How Sandra's first hugely successful business unexpectedly fell apart and the unlikely solution that helped her completely turn things around

- How Agnieszka almost gave up on love at the age of 40, thinking it just wasn't meant to be before she finally found the love of her life and how you can too

- How Angelique completely ignored the inner nudges of her soul and miraculously survived an earthquake before she finally owned her unique gifts

- How Magdalena overcame incredible odds by leaving her home country at the age of 19 and transformed from an anxiety-riddled introvert and unlikely leader to a pioneer in her industry

- How Daria was "sentenced" to battle an incurable autoimmune disease for the rest of her life and the unlikely discovery she made that helped her reverse the symptoms of the disease

- How Maggie's family concealed the painful truth from her and how she birthed her business on her father's deathbed while battling an autoimmune disease

- How Vindina went from defying nature, thinking she was "immortal" to having multiple-organ dysfunction before she finally found true healing

- How Monica finally mustered the courage to break free from a 30-year emotionally-abusive relationship and pursued her once-buried dreams

- How Sharan went against her cultural expectations, permanently uprooted limiting beliefs, and turned into a serial manifesting marvel that eventually led to marrying her soulmate

- How Alison, a mum of three, went from being overweight, feeling worthless, and believing she was a "burden" to completely transforming her body and her family's finances

If anything, our hope is that after reading this book you walk away feeling inspired and uplifted.

"At least my story wasn't as bad as hers."

CHAPTER 1:

A Book That Saved My Life

By Sandra Stachowicz

A series of seemingly unrelated devastating incidents spiralled out of control and brought me down to my knees about a year ago. As if by a stroke of magic, all my online marketing business ventures drew to a grinding halt, even though they had worked seamlessly for years. I could not comprehend what was happening!

In my mind, I was a veteran entrepreneur, yet I'd suffered a fatal stroke of fate which completely changed the trajectory of my business and life. These tragic incidents ensued within a few short months!

Literally, EVERYTHING I tried stopped working.

Completely out of the blue, business partners started pulling out one by one. Multiple sources of income that I had spent years building dried to a trickle, practically overnight. The fatal blow came when Google suspended my advertising account, accusing me of offences I did not commit.

I pulled my hair out of desperation, not fully understanding the scope of what was happening. At times, I wondered if I was bewitched or if invisible forces conspired against me.

I lost my sense of direction, but my bills didn't. I didn't know where to take my business next. At one point, I contemplated shutting all my online marketing operations down and taking time out for a year.

I had my "riches to rags" epiphany. Within weeks, I went from pulling in multiple high-end, four-figures per month to barely scraping by.

To an outsider, my success story from five years before happened practically overnight.

Within months, I went from being voluntarily enslaved at my 9-to-5 job to being the sought-out marketing expert. I was featured in a New York Times and Wall Street Journal bestseller. I published and co-authored an international bestselling book. I went on a six-month-long solo adventure and spent a few months working in exotic locations from the comfort of my laptop.

Soon enough, some of the biggest names in motivation and transformation circles reached out to work with me, including Sonia Ricotti, Debra Poneman, Marci Shimoff and many others. An opportunity of a lifetime presented itself when John Assaraf, best known from the film, *The Secret,* offered to promote me.

The fairy tale didn't last though, as shortly after co-authoring the international bestselling book, I changed my business direction. I effectively sealed my fate in the process as my lucky streak ran out just as abruptly.

With my tail tucked between my legs, I realised I needed to disappear to find myself again. I needed to take a step down from my business so I could clear my head and throw myself back into my entrepreneurial endeavours with renewed energy.

My friends, family, and followers thought I had given up. On the surface, it looked like all those years of entrepreneurship were wasted. Except that nothing is ever wasted.

Within six months, I had two full-time jobs working as a night manager for a holiday rental company and doubling as an Airbnb cleaner during the day. I worked seven days a week and didn't take any days off. I was tired. I was sleep-deprived. But I had a PLAN!

Between one sob and another, I realised that I could fail at a soul-sucking job that I didn't even want in the first place or I could fail at something I actually cared about for once! In the heat of the moment, I made up my mind to pursue a childish fantasy of mine that kept nudging me all those years.

Ever since I could read and write, I knew I wanted to become an author. When it became painfully obvious that my business was on the brink of a nervous breakdown, I turned into a woman on a mission and started setting the foundation to turn the impossible into possible and making my BIG childhood dream a reality.

Me, a girl from a post-communist country with broken English, the least likely author of them all.

Was I going to fail on an epic scale? Only time would tell.

I got to work straight away with the enthusiasm of a kid in a candy store and invested in a measly £3.33 e-book promising the secret to getting your book written and published.

I read it from cover to cover and immediately started implementing all the steps outlined in the book. I turned into a recluse with an Einstein-inspired look, and wrote like a mad scientist in a lab. Within days, I had 20k words worth of content.

Except that I still had no idea how to put all the missing puzzle pieces together and get published.

Fast forward six months, and I was pulling my hair out of desperation. As time went by, my hair was getting thinner but I still was nowhere near the publishing stage. With too many questions left unanswered, I frantically stared at a blank page, desperately searching for clues. As I soon discovered one-size-fits-all solutions provided in the e-book, while well-intended, failed to provide me with in-depth answers that would work for my book or my coaching business.

I desperately wanted to get my book out into the world but didn't have the ability to envision what steps I needed to take to get my book published and grow my coaching business through the book's success. I was pulled in a thousand directions by the demands of everyday life: needy partner, a marketing business that needed my undivided attention, and a stressful job.

Rather than getting my book published, I spun my wheels, getting nowhere. I felt constantly distracted by unfinished projects, the demands of running a business, bills that needed to be paid, and a partner and family who felt increasingly left out and neglected.

All I really wanted was to get my book out there and make an impact on the world, to succeed at something I actually loved!

I desperately tried to get my book completed, but ended up wearing too many different hats. I had to learn how keywords worked, grow my online presence, and be my own PR agent. All while making sure no one died in the process.

At one point I was so overwhelmed I almost gave up on writing altogether. Finally exhausted, I collapsed on the floor and exclaimed: "ENOUGH!"

Being the one-woman show that I am, I subscribed to the erroneous and deeply flawed belief that reaching out for help was a sign of weakness. To admit that I was somewhat lacking and didn't have the brains to figure out how to get my book written and printed was inconceivable in my mind and beyond painful.

I thought I was supposed to write my book on my own. But being "stuck on stupid" essentially kept me running in circles, with a book deadline that kept eluding me. Resigned, I concluded that if I was meant to write my book on my own, I would have published it already.

Then one New Year's Eve, I finally wised up.

When everyone was out and about celebrating and getting intoxicated as if there was no tomorrow, I was on the precipice of making one of the most important decisions in my life. As difficult as it was to acknowledge, I realised that unless I used a different approach, my half-finished manuscript would soon end up in a books' graveyard, in a pile of other almost-but-not-quite-finished projects in my desk drawer. Ouch!

Suddenly, as if struck by lightning, I had an 'aha' moment. "I've worked with up to five coaches at any one time to help me grow my coaching business. Why don't I hire a book coach to help me write and publish a book?"

Right in that moment, I made up my mind that this was the year I was going to get published. Period.

Without further ado, I put my money where my mouth was and entrusted all my savings to someone I barely knew, hiring a high-level book coach, one-to-one.

At last, I could put my energy where it belonged and pour all my heart, soul, and wine into what I loved the most, writing!

Or so I thought...

Deep down, I knew I was meant to write a book but caught myself thinking terrible thoughts about myself, my story, and my level of skill. As the villain of this story, from a remote village on the other side of the world and with less-than-impeccable English, I just didn't see myself as a gifted writer.

"You'll make a fool out of yourself. Who'd want to hear your story about your failed business or getting a lowly job most people would turn their nose to? There's nothing remarkable about you or your story."

"You're not exactly an authority in your niche. Look at you. You're a measly C-L-E-A-N-E-R. A wannabe author. An authority on water closets. How pathetic!"

I wrestled with my demons, but as if to confirm my inner dialogue, as I re-read the passage in my book where I effectively made a confession about my dirty little secret, an undercover stunt as a cleaner, and my eyes zoomed in on my editor's comments.

"What's so inspiring about having two full-time jobs?" There I had it. PROOF, highlighted in red. Tears welled up in my eyes and my heart just sunk.

"You see? Even your own editor doesn't believe you are enough of an expert. The one person who out of all the people in the world should have a little faith in the message of your book."

It became obvious, I was losing the argument. Score: 0-2 for the expert on water closets.

Except that my editor's remarks were completely innocent. They were taken out of context. I only saw what I wanted to see.

The closer I got to the launch date of my book, the more monsters that crawled out from under my bed: doubt, shame, guilt, and fear. Out of desperation I turned to my book coach for guidance. "I can't do this! I'm not enough of an expert!"

I ended up borrowing my book coach's belief in me when I didn't have any left in myself.

Having him in my corner meant I had a Sherpa guiding me through the treacherous terrain of becoming a published bestselling author. Re-assured by my coach, I made peace with my own "not enoughness," safe in the knowing that my book was coming out exactly as it should.

Still, something else quietly robbed me of the joy of getting my book published, preventing me from pouring all my heart and soul into my book. I couldn't quite reconcile my love for writing with being voluntarily enslaved in a soul-sucking job.

I secretly wished it was as simple as handing in my notice but losing my job essentially meant a death sentence for my book. As often is with all matters of substance, once you make up your mind, the Universe conspires behind the scenes to answer your prayers.

To my utter surprise, I realised I had accrued unspent holidays at my job. I had not been on holiday for over a year and yearned for a three-week-long summer break in a tropical destination with my long-term boyfriend.

Still, the deadly shadow of my book's launch date loomed over me. As I got closer to the publishing stage, I realised I needed to dedicate myself fully to my book, with no distractions whatsoever. Chasing down my dream of becoming a published bestselling author was either now or never.

I knew I had to make one of the most difficult decisions ever, even if this choice meant letting my partner down. To my colleagues' and bosses' dismay, rather than spend hundreds of pounds on holidays in some exotic location, I spent the following three weeks at my home in rainy Scotland, tucked away under duvets, perfecting the script of my book.

The sacrifices paid off. Half a month later, the script was ready! But I still wasn't. Yet I had to return to work, just as enthusiastic about it as a child being asked to apologize for eating the last cookie.

A few weeks before my book was published, my fancy job promotion from night-manager to content-manager unexpectedly fell through and I found myself jobless. The burden of unpaid bills loomed over me. My dream of ever becoming a published author was suddenly at stake.

I unexpectedly had 40 hours of time each week freed up but I was effectively liberated from the main source of income too. With losing my job, came another dilemma.

I could potentially waste precious hours applying for temporary jobs just to tie me over or completely commit to writing and potentially risk not having enough money left over to pay my editor.

It finally dawned on me that everything I spent the last few months working on could effectively put the launch of my book on hold until "someday," sealing my book's fate in the process and ensuring that my book would never see daylight.

Not now, not ever.

Admittedly, after my promotion suddenly fell through, I was at my wits end, frustrated beyond words, resentful, and upset. Still, some people seem to have a knack for knocking others when they are down. My mum has built-in receptors to pick up on those rare moments with stunning accuracy.

During one of her visits my mother probed pitilessly, "What if you fail? Will you pack up and move back home with me?"

I just looked at her without uttering a word, too taken aback to speak up. Tears welled up in my eyes. I felt hurt.

Failing was simply NOT an option!

If anything, my mother's off-handed remark made me realize that up until that moment I hadn't really gone ALL-IN with my book or my coaching business.

The reason my business wasn't working for me was because I wasn't working for it. Rather than make my mother's unflattering comments mean anything about me, I threw myself back into entrepreneurial endeavours with renewed energy.

For me, publishing a book wasn't a matter of, "How do I make money?" it was a matter of, "How do I get back up to the standard of living I am used to making?"

This sudden realisation led to an unlikely epiphany. "Just because I failed does not make me a failure. Why don't I leverage that idea and build up on my failures?!" With sudden clarity, I realised not all was lost and I could lean on my previous successes, just as much as I could draw strength from my failures.

After months of hard work and with my fingers trembling, I finally hit publish, and got my transformational book out into the world, anxiously refreshing my Amazon listing every five minutes.

To my utter surprise, getting my book published worked like a charm as I landed my first few coaching clients before my book even officially launched and had a bestselling-author status under my belt. I turned a seemingly devastating experience into a massive win as I had one of the best months I've had to date!

Et voilà! A recipe for a hugely successful coaching business on steroids.

In hindsight, getting my book published was the best plan ever.

These days my book does the heavy lifting for me as I wake up to new subscribers, booked discovery calls, and email payment notifications. Potential clients literally turn up on my doorstep. Sometimes I wonder where the magic wand was hiding during all those lean years!

These days I inject the passion for writing into every woman I come into contact with. I spread the contagion by shaking their hearts up and making them hang their insides on the outside. I whack them in the head with the uncomfortable truth and make them cough up soul-aligned books, totally guilt-free.

I am on a mission to help women coaches get their transformational bestselling book written and published in 90 days or less so they can finally have the breakthrough they waited for during all those lean years. I gently guide them to get their book out of their soul and out into the world so they can effortlessly scale their business to six figures and beyond, without working 13-hour days, following every marketing strategy out there, or losing themselves in the process.

Nowadays, I see myself as a freedom fixer, I give women back what is rightfully theirs: time. The freedom to just be, without the heavy price tag.

Looking back, if I hadn't bet on myself and published my book, I honestly don't think I'd still have a coaching business.

I most certainly would not be here sitting on my favourite fallen tree over a creek, with a grin on my face, my feet dangling, dipping my big toe in a cold-water stream, and clutching the latest copy of my client's book.

As I think back to the time before I got my book published, I wasn't following my dreams, I only thought I was. I just dipped my big toe in to test the waters, hoping that one day the world would find out what a best-kept secret I was! I wasn't truly chasing my childhood dream of becoming an author. And I effectively stalled my business growth by not listening to the inner nudges of my soul that gently whispered, "Go, get that book of yours published."

I told myself terrible untruths that my dream of one day becoming a published author could wait until "someday." What I didn't realise is that "someday" could have easily turned into "never," and with that, my hope of ever re-activating my coaching business.

Unbeknownst to me, my business falling apart set me on the path towards exponential growth as I reconciled my passion for writing and finally got my transformational book published.

Equipped with newly-found wisdom, I realised that business doesn't have to be a struggle. Business can be easy, but only if you let it.

Having a bestselling author status is the easiest way to live life. My book not only saved my business. It saved my life. It salvaged my sanity as an entrepreneur.

Books have the power to change the trajectory of your business and life. You can publish a book once and reap the rewards for years to come.

To my surprise, publishing a book provided me with the never-ending sense of adventure, freedom, and meaning. Sometimes I feel as if I opened a Pandora 's Box full of surprises and unleashed a whole plethora of unexpected opportunities. Who would have ever believed that my book would be placed by the bedsides in the Waldorf Astoria, the very same hotel that I once worked for as a cleaner?

The guilty pleasures of life!

They say, build it and they will come. I say, write it and they will come. And come they will. In hoards.

Sandra Stachowicz is a book coach for women coaches, an international bestselling author, and the founder of *Awaken Inner Goddess* - which takes a decidedly different view on how business books should be written and published.

She is on a mission to help spiritual and unconventional women coaches get their first book out of their soul and into the world in 90 days so they can exponentially grow their heart-centred businesses, get fully booked with high-end clients, and embark on a round-the-world, never-ending adventure. She works with passionate women, out-of-the-box thinkers, visionaries, soul-fuelled coaches, mentors, and healers who want to expand their souls and bank accounts while making an impact.

She is a free spirit, psychic, introvert, gypsy-at-heart and she loves talking about herself in third-person. Most of all, she believes our stories have the power to heal. Her desire is to heal the world one soul, one book at a time.

Sandra built three businesses by the age of 30. She wrote *Leap Afraid: How to Turn a Devastating Series of Events into the Best Thing That Ever Happened to You,* which instantly became a bestseller and also co-authored the international bestseller, *Rising Above.* Her story was featured in a New York Times and Wall Street

Journal bestselling book that shared how inspiring women escaped their 9-to-5 jobs and became successful entrepreneurs.

Are you ready to finally get that book of yours written and published? Take the first step towards becoming a published bestselling author now and grab your complimentary copy of *The Ultimate Guide to Writing Business Books for Women Coaches: How to Write a Best-Selling Book in 30 Days or Less (Without Any Previous Writing Experience)* by clicking here https://leapafraid.com/wild.

Stop spinning your wheels and getting nowhere. Get your bestselling book written and published in less than 90 days and scale your coaching business to six figures and beyond!

CHAPTER 2:

Reclaiming Myself

By Monica Linson

It felt as though the room was spinning. The sour taste and burning feel of vomit reached the back of my throat. As I sat there listening, I knew what I was hearing. I understood the words, but nothing he said seemed to make any sense.

I was the one who wanted out of the toxicity. I wanted to be free of his lies, his infidelity, and the silent treatment that came whenever his ego was bruised. More than that, I wanted to be free of having to walk on eggshells or the deafening loneliness. That's why I had asked him to leave.

Now here I was, sucked back in with his promises to go to therapy consistently, to finally accept that he needed help. For months, he had scoured the internet for new wedding bands with the intent of renewing our vows. He made so many plans, so many promises. I forgave. I believed.

Now, he wanted out of our 30-year marriage. Like everything else that went wrong in his life, he blamed me for his lack of joy, ease, and lightness. Apparently, dating other women provided this fulfillment. He said that the adrenaline rush that came with the idea was something he simply couldn't shake. I was the one thing in the way.

To justify his decision, he added, "For God's sake Monica, I can't even get it up with you anymore! Just look at you." On and on he went, blaming me and excusing himself as he reminded me of betrayals that I didn't want to remember, events for which he once feigned remorse. "I don't think I did anything wrong. I just apologized because I was just trying to be the good guy. You're too sensitive," he said. Oh, how his words cut me!

While I had gained weight with each pregnancy and no longer weighed the 130 pounds of our wedding day, I continued to put forth an effort to look attractive and stay fit. Up until that moment, I believed I had been successful. Later, when my rational mind was present, I had the good sense to know that his words were simply projections of what he felt about himself. I even had moments of righteous anger. After all, his physical appearance had been hit harder by time than mine. His receding hair line gave way to balding from his forehead well into the crown, save a few wisps of hair on the top. I was grateful that he kept them cut very close to keep from looking like Bozo the Clown.

As far as his not being able to get it up with me, I knew the truth. The doctor had explained that erectile dysfunction was a common experience for a man his age. In fact, the doctor provided pamphlets explaining that half of all men in their 50's were affected by mild to moderate ED. Somehow these realities escaped both of us. In his eyes, I was to blame for his erectile dysfunction. At one time, I saw his condition as something that we would navigate together. But in that moment, I couldn't stop the brain chatter that also blamed me. Where once I felt gratitude and pride in my body for the ability to conceive and carry two difficult pregnancies to term, all I could see was proof of my guilt — stretch marks, loose skin, and deflated breasts.

In the weeks following his departure, sleep chased me. I ran from it in order to avoid dreams that replayed the night my world imploded. During the day, my primary goal was to remain upright and not become unglued in public. At the end of each work day, the moment I reached the safety of my car, my resolve would break. The tears that burned just behind my eyes all day flowed freely. Guttural wails came from somewhere deep inside me. I was sure that my crying could be heard by the drivers in passing cars.

Throughout the day and night, my body vacillated between shaking uncontrollably and feeling as if it was on fire. Stabbing pains seared my heart each time I caught sight of a small red car, in fear that it might be him. Within a short time, my life became foreign to me. The man that I spent so many years loving, the man who professed to love me and who wanted to renew our wedding vows just three weeks previously was now the person I needed to protect myself from.

It didn't seem to matter that I had supported him through graduate school nor that I was the one who kept him afloat when his first attempt at a private practice failed. I was the one who helped build his clientele as an associate in another practice. I also encouraged him to leap at the chance to try again at private practice. I even helped him rebrand the company image. It was my salary that kept a roof over our heads and food on the table while the practice grew. So, why did the man, whom I believed was the love of my life, declare himself my enemy? Why was he so determined to destroy me?

The assaults continued! In the same conversation, my soon-to-be-ex acknowledged that he shouldn't have blamed me for his erectile dysfunction and also asked me if I wanted the Sleep Number mattress, an expensive model that I purchased with the money from my side hustle as a licensed massage therapist. But he also 'needed' to let me know that he slept with other women on the mattress. Repeatedly, he disguised himself as the caring, thoughtful, generous, funny, bumbling innocent that I first met. Then without warning, he turned on me.

During this time when we were supposedly working out an amicable dissolution of our marriage, the man I loved accused me of hiding money and of not being trustworthy to pay our sons' college expenses as promised. Therefore, the money that I supposedly hid, along with the money earmarked for tuition, was counted among my assets. This same man also played the victim, as if his hands were tied, by letting me know that his accountant had to adjust the business taxes so that it appeared that his private practice yielded less than my teacher's salary. The underlying threat was that I could end up paying him alimony. None of his statements made any sense! This newest version of my then-husband seemed deliberately cruel and incapable of doing basic math.

The constant accusations all took a heavy toll on my health. I was battered and bruised, emotionally and mentally! My life dwindled to merely existing. Sleep. Eat. Work. Repeat. Every other week, I sought the support of a therapist.

Then one day, as I was driving along, minding my own business, I received a message. Whether it was by way of Divine intervention or strong intuition, I am not sure. But the voice delivering the message was strong and clear. "This is not the first time you've heard this diagnosis," I distinctly heard. I glanced in the rearview mirror for evidence of a forgotten passenger, yet no one was there.

I drove faster as if to distance myself from the disembodied voice in my backseat. I heard the words "Breathe... Breathe!" I drove faster still. "Diagnosis?" I asked out loud. With that simple question, the recall was instant. No less than six times, the man I loved had been identified as a narcissist or diagnosed with Narcissistic Personality Disorder. The faces of past mental health therapists, flooded my memory. Yet I questioned, had they told me the whole story? What did the diagnosis have to do with his behavior now?

I'd followed all of their recommendations on how to deal with the disorder. I understood what they told me about his Rock-Star Mentality. I made a big deal when he walked through the door each evening and taught our kids to do the same. I didn't take every arrogant comment he made personally. In fact, I got very good at ignoring his patronizing tone, giving him the benefit of the doubt.

Yet that night, when I typed the word narcissist into GOOGLE, over 70 million results popped up. I read article after article. There, recorded in black-and-white, was my life. I learned that I had been targeted and then love bombed. This information confirmed that I had not imagined that the man I loved seemed so very different at the start of our relationship. The abuse cycle of love bombing, devaluing, and discarding explained why the nice-guy, the man I first met, appeared at different times, just to leave again.

I read about the traits of narcissists, which exceeded the Rock-Star Mentality that was previously offered as a definition. I found that narcissists display grandiosity and a need for undue admiration. They feel a sense of superiority and believe social rules do not apply to them. Narcissists lack empathy and are only able to view matters from their vantage point. They lack accountability for their actions, and are hypersensitive to any criticism that stands in contrast to the false image they hold of themselves. Narcissists need power and control. They have a strong sense of entitlement, believing that they deserve any and all that they want.

I also read about the tactics of gas-lighting, silent-treatments, and the appearance of 'Dr. Jekyll and Mr. Hyde.' There, laid before me on my computer screen, was documented proof that countless women and I lived parallel lives. I found this fact both comforting and alarming. I was comforted because I felt validated. I hadn't imagined all the inconsistencies in my relationship and I wasn't the only one who had been duped by a narcissist. The alarming part was that most of the women whose experiences I read were still lost, still in pain, still plagued by confusion and bitterness ten to fifteen years after the end of their relationships.

As I continued my research, anger, confusion, and despair surfaced. The voice was right! I had heard the diagnosis before. But what the mental health professionals who informed me that the man I loved is a narcissist didn't tell me was just how insidious, dangerous, and permanent the disorder is. Why didn't they tell me? How had I not seen this all before? Why did I try so hard to help someone who couldn't be helped?

I was led to believe that with patience, support, and love, a narcissist could change. Yet, everything I read indicated the opposite. A narcissist cannot change. They lack the ability to reflect on their own behavior and the wiring in their brain will not allow them to truly acknowledge personal faults. This same wiring makes the narcissist incapable of truly loving another person.

Determined to not be controlled any longer, I set about to reclaim myself! I learned all I could about recovering from emotional and mental abuse. I learned that the bodily sensations I experienced of insomnia, uncontrollable trembling, and a burning-skin feeling were responses to trauma. I finally processed the buried emotions that resulted from trying to keep a semblance of peace in my marriage by feeding my husband's narcissist ego.

My sudden irrational fear of small red cars was linked to C-PTSD. I simply couldn't reconcile that the person who claimed to love me was one and the same with the person who had become crueler than I thought possible and who replaced me within weeks of our separation. I feared running into him face-to-face. Yet, at times he was the very person I hoped would rescue and comfort me. Trauma bonding, also known as Stockholm syndrome, explained the desire to seek comfort in the arms of the very person who inflicted my wounds. It was clear to me that the road to recovery was going to take real and consistent effort.

Self-care became a priority. I needed to get well, which meant supporting my body as it processed the trauma. Naps, long soaks in the tub, massage, and solitude became staples of my life. I sought the expertise of energy workers: Reiki; Pranic, and Theta Healing; as well as Shamanic journeying. I became certified in Reiki and Sound Healing, and I studied Shamanism all in the effort to take command of my recovery. I studied courses on Theta Healing to reprogram subconscious beliefs and release trapped emotions. I sought hypnotherapy to shift my limiting beliefs and pursued certification in the subject, as well.

Inner-child work was crucial to my recovery from narcissistic abuse. We establish the lens in which we see the world very early in life. I forced myself to examine all of my core beliefs, to ask and answer the tough questions. Through my research, I discovered that my father, although undiagnosed, also fit all of the criteria of a covert narcissist. Having been raised by a narcissist, I was primed and conditioned to marry one. I was programmed to put others' needs before my own, to accept the blame and responsibility for problems that I didn't create, and to forgive and forget many egregious offenses. More significantly, I came to realize that I had watched my mother feed my father's ego and gained that skill myself. As a youngster, I learned to play the toxic relationship game. I simply didn't know that it was toxic.

I applied all that I learned about Narcissistic Personality Disorder and recognized how being enmeshed with narcissists impacted my life. I assessed where I stood in all major areas of my life, including physical, mental, and emotional health, finances, relationships, etc. I created a plan to reclaim my life and followed it. Within six months, I was grounded in a new chapter of my life. But the journey was tough! There were tears of grief and frustration! There was screaming and pillow-punching! There were also breakthroughs and celebrations.

It's funny that those moments of success also brought tears, but tears of joy and hope!

Although I believe that my journey is far from over, I knew that I had made it to the other side of my recovery when I awoke with giggles and excitement for the day, when I set and enforced personal boundaries, and when I was able to bless every small red car that I passed! The greatest indication of my successful recovery is that I now can trust my inner voice, that intuition and gut feeling that I ignored for far too long. I no longer live in fear or on high alert. I have peace of mind. Most days I am happy for no particular reason - just because I'm here!

I now harness all my experience, knowledge, and determination to support other women (and a few men) in recovering from narcissistic-abusive relationships. I support survivors in understanding the disorder and making sense of their own experiences. I've found that it takes someone who has lived with narcissism to truly understand what such a toxic relationship entails. Through one-on-one or group coaching, I provide the tools and strategies needed to navigate the emotional and mental aftermath of a narcissistically-abusive relationship. People who work with me reclaim their sanity, clarity, and hope which then empowers them to not simply survive, but to thrive!

If you feel that you are stuck in your recovery from a narcissistically-abusive relationship or any toxic relationship, then I'd be honored to support you. I am confident that I can assist you in creating your map to recovery and a fabulous new life. You don't deserve the abuse. You have the power to recover and reclaim yourself! You deserve to be whole and happy! And I'll be with you every step of the way!

Contact me at my website:
https://ReclaimingYourselfNow.com;

or through email at monica@ReclaimingYourselfNow.com

XOXO,

Monica

Monica Linson is your guide to reclaiming your SANITY, CLARITY, and HOPE after a toxic relationship of narcissistic abuse. Monica thought the day that her marriage to a covert narcissist imploded was the worst day of her life. But she now celebrates the third of each month as her Liberation Day! Monica reclaimed herself by healing the psychological, emotional, spiritual, and sexual wounds that resulted from the abuse. After navigating the fallout, she realized that she was finally free of the pain, confusion, and FOG (fear, obligation, and guilt) that comes with being bound to a covert narcissist.

Monica was actually raised by a narcissist, which left her primed to marry one. Feeling at home with the dysfunction, she mistook familiarity for love. She often says that she learned to play the 'please-the-narcissist' game well. She simply wasn't aware that the game was toxic and quite deadly for many others.

Her mission now is to support thousands of women to thrive after narcissistic abuse. Monica provides private coaching as well as a group coaching course called *Reclaiming Yourself Now*. Monica allows women who are still shifting through the shambles of their relationship with a narcissist to make sense of the experience, find their power in the pain, set and enforce boundaries, heal childhood wounds, and create a fabulous future. She's working on her self-help book, *The Covert Narcissist* and the *Reclaiming Yourself Now Journal*, both in progress.

If Monica's mission resonates with you, or you would simply like to know more, feel free to contact her at
https://ReclaimingYourselfNow.com

or on Facebook at
https://www.facebook.com/Reclaiming.Yourself.Now/

As a gift, you are invited to shift all of your unhealthy relationship dynamics by taking the course, "10 Steps to Ending Toxic Relationships." Use the code: WILDWOMEN.

CHAPTER 3:

The Life-Changing Journey of an Ordinary Girl

By Angelique Mol

As long as I remember, I always felt different. Different from other children, but also an outsider within my own family. As a child I always felt that I didn't fit in. I also was somewhat of a loner. I didn't need many friends around me but I was not really good at making loads of friends either. I felt a tinge of jealousy at the other kids who seemed to have multiple friends, while my only friends were mainly furry and four-legged, namely horses. Through a friend I ended up at a local stable where I was able to look after and care for a horse on a daily basis. There I learned dressage and participated in some local competitions. I basically spent most of my free time outside of school at the stables where I felt most comfortable. At school I was bullied, probably because I felt I was different. I was not the kind of girl that was popular, so I never fit in. While with the horses I felt safe and I was not bullied by others at the stables.

My home and family situation were not ideal either. Even there I felt quite alone. If there was a black sheep in the family, it was definitely me. I always wanted my choices to be different because I enjoyed different interests than most of my family. But most of the time, I was expected to do as I was told and exactly how to do it, whether I liked it or not. Eventually, I started to feel more comfortable in being alone and spending time on my own in my room. I didn't get the support from my family I needed and always tried to solve problems myself, finding my own way in basically every area. My father was an alcoholic but my mum always tried her hardest to give my brother and me the best home life that she could, despite the constant financial struggle. I never wanted to take friends home because I felt ashamed about my father and never told anyone about his problems. There was often tension and arguments so I felt I needed to deal with my problems and emotions on my own.

Then there were the expectations on how life should be and how I should live my life: finish school, get a job, find a boyfriend, get married, have children. I was raised to believe that these accomplishments were what life was about. Not knowing any better, I felt I had no other choice than to do as I was told and live my life how my family and society decided I should. To live my life according the expectations of others. I felt that I had no choice but to meet those expectations.

Believe me, I reached a point where I had no idea what to do with my life. I couldn't see how I could change my situation, my circumstances, or my direction. Sometimes I wished I had the courage to just pack my things and leave. Leave my home situation and be free, released from the expectations of my family and society in general. The Wild Woman inside of me wanted to break free, but I just didn't have the courage or even the knowledge of how to take back my life. What might my family say if I decided to pack up and leave, freeing myself from the bird cage where I felt trapped by expectations? I still felt that I needed their approval about how I should live my life and what I ought to do.

I followed their advice, "You are here to finish your schooling, get a job, get your driver's license, get married, and have children." At first, I was happy to some extent with my marriage and my daughter, but there remained this deep urge to make more of my life than what I had. I couldn't name what that desire was, but it boiled inside me like a slow cooker. I always knew that at some point that force would rise up to the surface; the only question was...when?

I found a starting point that allowed me to break free from expectations when I set up a beauty business even though some people thought it would not work out. I decided to follow my heart and make it successful. Within ten years I build up my business and managed to open two salons in different cities. Yet my home life was not ideal, so when my marriage ended, I felt the need to step away from everything in order to reflect on my life and what I wanted to do with it. I knew that my life needed more purpose.

Finally, the boiling point rose to the surface! The moment arrived when I was so fed up with my ordinary life that I had to get out, leave, run, flee! I received the opportunity to work in a different country which felt like a "now or never" chance. Take it now, or leave it and regret it later in your life. So, I decided to let the Wild Woman in me come out and I went for this opportunity, despite what other people said or thought about it. I imagined that fantastic moment, finally breaking free from my family restraints, making my own decisions without having to ask for "permission" or "approval." That thought made me jump for joy and I could literally not wait until the day arrived for me to get on a plane and start my Wild Woman journey! I felt like I was leaving behind everything that ensnared me and cutting cords with my past.

The moment I got off the plane, I felt like I was home...New Zealand! All the way from the Netherlands, I literally travelled to the other side of the world, yet it felt safe, far away from everything and everyone. With only a suitcase of clothes and about 1000 Euros in pocket money, I started a new life, together with my daughter. She has always been part of my journey and is a great companion and friend. I didn't know anyone in New Zealand except for a Dutch couple I got in touch with through a blogpost they shared about moving to New Zealand. They inspired me even more to start a new life.

I had a job lined up in a salon to work as a beauty therapist, as my previous experience gave me the best opportunity to get a work visa. I also had sorted out a place to live before we left the Netherlands. For the first three weeks, we lived in a temporary home while arranging a more permanent place. I ended up finding us a house in the hills with stunning New Zealand views. About six months later, we moved again to a more rural area with a house that had a fantastic view over vineyards.

This was the life! Every aspect of my new life was fantastic! I was free, had a good job, lived in a stunning country, and met some great Spiritual people. I had always felt a spiritual pull on my life and tried to discover more about what resonated with me, but had never found a clear and direct path. But in New Zealand, I delved into more spiritual practices like healing, meditation, and card readings. These practices confirmed that my move was all meant to be and definitely a part of the reason why I ended up half-way across the world. I felt as if nothing could go wrong.

Then the news came from my employer. I could not extend my current work permit since the government wanted my employer to hire local people instead of immigrants. The world suddenly sank down under my feet. This situation was not happening. It could not be happening! I wanted to settle down in my new country, to live with her for the rest of my life! But without a work permit I would have to leave.

I didn't give up, of course! I would simply not allow myself to return home, as this country was home now! Nowhere else felt as much like home as New Zealand! I felt safe and comfortable, surrounded by lovely, like-minded people and amazing surroundings. So, in the little time I had left before my work permit expired, I applied for jobs in the same field, as that was my best chance to get another job elsewhere in New Zealand. Quite quickly, I managed to get an interview in Christchurch, which was a four-hour drive from where I lived. But the job opening felt like the only chance I had to stay in New Zealand, so I travelled the eight-hour round trip for a 30-minute interview. Thankfully, I got the job and could start nearly straight away. I was saved, for the time being.

I packed up my possessions and my daughter again and moved to Christchurch. I could continue working towards to applying for permanent residency one day, and life felt great again! First, my work permit needed to be processed but I had a good connection with my employer. I again met some nice, wonderful people. I had a lovely little house and life felt back on track again.

I also focused more on spiritual work and my own spiritual personal development which started to feel more and more like my Life Purpose. I was drawn to healing practices and discovered that I have the natural gift of healing when I helped a friend with cluster headaches. I did more self-study about healing and practised on other people who confirmed they could feel the results. I finally realised that I knew my life's purpose and how I could truly help people. I could not imagine that anything could go wrong at this point but the Universe obviously had other plans for me...

It hit hard and suddenly. A big, 6.3-magnitude Earthquake. I was at work around lunch time when the roaring sound of the Earth made me realise something really bad was happening. The rumbling got more and more intense and the room started to shake. I couldn't move but knew I needed to make my way to the doorway, where it was safer from falling items and building collapse. Products, bottles, and frames fell off the shelves and walls. The sensation was like being on a ship in a terrible storm. The floor moved like massive waves. As everyone screamed, I finally made it to the doorway. It was very frightening!

When at last the earthquake subsided, we all quickly made our way outside to witness the damage that Mother Earth created. Streets were ripped open, water bubbled up from underneath the concrete, little shops had totally collapsed. And we, we were all in shock. What just happened? And what would happen next?

Because of this tragic event, many people lost their homes; some people even lost their lives. And I could no longer stay in New Zealand. The premises where I worked were so damaged that they had to close for a long time to rebuild and refurbish. While the shop was closed, I could not keep my work permit. I could not believe that my dream, to live my life in New Zealand where I finally found my purpose had to come to an end, after living there for just over two years.

But I am a strong believer of when circumstances are meant to be or not, so I accepted that this ending must be a part of my journey. A good friend of mine, a spiritual medium, gave me the peace of mind that I was obviously needed elsewhere to fulfill my Purpose.

I ended up in Belgium and for a year I operated a pub/cafe with someone who I considered a friend when we started the business. But this choice ended disastrously as well. I could have chosen to see that situation as a failure, but instead I tried to view it as another learning moment. Still, within myself, I knew there was more for me to do, something better, something more meaningful.

I had this inner yearning to know more about helping people through healing practices and so I continued to invest in myself. I found comfort in studying healing in herbalism. I began to make herbal remedies and dedicated myself to life-long learning by qualifying as a Reiki master and shamanic healing practitioner. Both Reiki and shamanic healing are forms of energy healing. With Reiki healing, you work as a vessel for life-force energy to help people heal physically, emotionally, or mentally. Shamanic healing allows you to focus more with the cause or root of the problem through past-life healing, soul retrieval, DNA healing, power retrieval, or removing misplaced energies or entities.

The healing practices I learned during this part of my journey allow me to help people with deep issues, which is so fulfilling! And I finally came to the realisation that the places I've been, the people I've met, and all the experiences I've gone through were all part of my journey towards my Soul Purpose. This purpose is to help people, care for animals, and make a difference in the world. I got introduced to animal healing once I studied Reiki healing, so I continued studying animal and equine Reiki healing, which is especially designed for horses. All the events in my life, the good ones, and especially the challenging ones, gave me so much clarity. Now, more than ever, I know what I have to do. I finally understand what I came here to do and it is time to get on with it!

I help people and animals by providing healing treatments and herbal remedies for all different kinds of ailments, whether on a physical, emotional, mental or spiritual level. Energy healing helps to heal the body in a natural way without any side effects, even when people are under medical supervision. People from all walks of life benefit from alternative healing which uses natural alternatives to pharmaceutical options. I have experienced so many positive results and feedback from clients, and that's why I love doing this work. Knowing that I help people heal within and feel better with a positive attitude about life again, makes me feel good within myself. That is the most important reward I can get from this work.

I grew up as a shy, insecure girl, always trying to make other people happy, not realising that I had the right to make my own life, my own choices, my own dreams and goals. Over the years, I developed myself through my experiences and studies to become a strong, independent Wild Woman because I decided, "No more!" No more living my life for other people but only for myself, no more explaining to others why or why not, and no more making other people happy rather than myself.

What I learned during my journey is that no one can stop you from doing what you want to do, what you feel deep down that you need to do. The only one who can stop you from fulfilling your Soul Purpose, is you. I previous lived my life according to other's expectations, but that life was so unfulfilled and unbearable that I had no other choice than to leave and break free. Looking back, I allowed myself to stay stuck and unfulfilled for way too long; I should have made the decision to escape much earlier in my life. But I have no regrets either, for each occurrence happened just how it was supposed to for me. All the events I went through were lessons and I learned that you can find your purpose if you are willing to go for it. Becoming independent so I could grow and develop within myself and learning to make my own choices were the most important decisions I ever made.

It's important to find your own Purpose, why you are here and what you are meant to do. You don't have to try to fit other's expectations. In the end, it's your life to live, so make sure you can look back on your life one day and be proud of everything you have achieved. Don't take your life for granted or just accept your circumstances simply because they are comfortable or because you feel like you have to make other people happy. Take your life in your own hands, find your purpose, and choose what you would love to do. Then, dare to break free from the bird cage that holds you back, just like I did. If I can change my life and find my soul purpose, so can you!

Stop doubting that you can change your life but start working towards that change. Don't wait until the "right time" as there is no right time; there is only the time that you decide for yourself to make a change. Become the person you are meant to become. Be driven but have patience. Change might not happen overnight, but if you set out your intentions and focus on your goals, dreams, and purpose, you will awaken the Wild Woman in you.

Angelique Mol is a Reiki Master, Herbalist, Shamanic Healing Practitioner, and Holistic Life Coach who assists her clients in finding inner peace, balance, and happiness through her Holistic Life Coaching. Her Soul Purpose and mission is to use Energy Healing Treatments for both people and animals. She also operates *Healing and Herbs, Ltd*, an online healing shop that specializes in healing items, herbs, and remedies.

She started to feel a bit more like a Gypsy and Free Spirit once she moved a few times to different countries to do her work and to follow her dreams and Soul Purpose. Born in the Netherlands, she has also spent time in New Zealand and Belgium. She now resides in the United Kingdom. She met a lot of fantastic people everywhere she lived, but also had the chance to help people within her Soul Mission.

She is a free, Wild Woman who strives to pursue her dreams and manifest them for the Greater Good.

If you want to create a better and healthier life for yourself and want to feel more happiness, inner peace, and in balance within yourself and your life, Angelique can help you release old attachments and energies so you can move forward. If you feel stuck and lost, then book a FREE consultation with

Angelique by clicking on the following link:
www.healingandherbs.com/free-offers

or connect with her on Facebook:
www.facebook.com/HealingandHerbs

CHAPTER 4:

How I Turned a Living Burial into a Blooming Germination

By Vindina Mitha

Food buried my life vision. And for 30 years, I didn't realize that I was steadily fast-tracking my way to the grave until I landed up for a two-week vacation... in the hospital. There I was pumped full of morphine because my medical team couldn't figure out what was wrong with my body.

For over a week, I lay in a hospital bed, subjected to MRI's, spinal taps, and arrays of invasive procedures to diagnose my symptoms. Splitting headaches, nausea, vomiting, imbalance, inability to walk. Intolerance to light and sound. An endless list.

My symptoms had developed gradually. They started as annoying hindrances that made me a miserable grouch but quickly became overwhelming within a few, very short weeks. Overwhelming to the point that I migrated from frustrated and anxious to uneasy, scared, and worried as my episodes gained in frequency and intensity.

The progression was so fast, so cantankerous, that within weeks, every morning I gingerly opened my right eye a peek to test the day before I reached for earplugs, sunglasses, eye mask, and drawn blackout curtains. If I didn't, the light overwhelmed me and I was sucked into a vortex of debilitating pain so that I had to remain isolated, in a darkened bedroom.

In the aftermath, between episodes I could hear better, see better, and walk unaided but I was left physically and emotionally drained and non-functional. Rattled. Trying to piece together the past few days of delirium.

Living this cycle of cringing from morning light to reassembling my days around health limitations was enough for me to know that something was fundamentally wrong.

I trusted my specialist but I wanted a quick fix, which consisted of daily, then weekly, then monthly injections, as well as weekly pills.

I got a list of rules from my stint in hospital. Eat these foods, avoid those. You will be fine. I also got a finger wag from my doc and specialist. Self-care, slow down, take time, rest up, be kinder to yourself... on and on.

I didn't really want to change. I just wanted superglue to hold my life together. I wanted to continue in pre-illness health.

Even though I was paralyzed in fear at times and didn't want to stay with this new trajectory of uncertainty, hopelessness, and terror, as my body healed, my mind got fickle.

My memories of being more scared of the constant needles than my life-long snake phobia faded and I got used to new norms.

Eventually, I carried on with old habits and incorporated very few new ones.

Before I knew it, there I was in relapse. My total body revolt was back. Only a year later, I was back to being Countess Dracula. I just needed a coffin for the week I lay in isolation at the hospital.

Again, the poignancy didn't escape me – illness wasn't my agenda. I was barely halfway through my life!

The question is: when is illness ever on anyone's agenda? Have you experienced the creaks, aches, and pains that suddenly hinge on a tipping point?

And what about the annual medical result with its diagnosis? And then you have that change, mostly drastic.

Have you been booked in for a specialist appointment? Followed by a procedure?

And what about that recovery period that is now longer than a weekend so you run at half-steam the week afterwards?

How about your mental performance slowing down? Brain Fog. When you're not as quick on the take.

And we keep thinking that all this degradation is normal. We think it's normal for us to bury our life's visions because we become limited by the creaks, pains, diagnoses, procedures. We accept becoming slower and not performing as we used to. Don't we?

During my week in hospital, I again contemplated my old trajectory and realised that my ground zero was bleak. I needed a magic lamp to rub. Straws to clutch. Anything. Because symptomatic treatment was not going to work for me. Clearly, neither was the conventional food list and finger wag from the doctors.

Within weeks, I took the step and made the decision for a revolutionary health reprogramming. I had thought about this reprogram since my hospital stint a year before. But there was always gawd-awful timing. Every excuse not to take care of my greatest wealth.

Projects. Work always came first.

Travels. I was always on the go.

Holidays. I had time but there was too much to eat through. So not a good time for a foodie.

Money. Ah yes, such a big excuse. There was always something else that needed attention. As if two weeks in hospital, medical excesses, and chronic medical care weren't costly.

But this time, my burial was deep. I refused to go back to cringing at every new day. Nor the intermittent life-drain between episodes. I wasn't rechargeable. And it showed.

This time, however, there was ACTUAL totally inconvenient timing. It was the last quarter of the financial year. And I had the lab data in hand for the real fun part of research.

But this time, my health trumped any last-quarter shenanigans. Recurring illness, life-long symptomatic treatment, and more than 20 kilograms overweight in my early 30's trumped any universal shenanigans.

This reprogramming was my magic lamp and the genie was still in residence! The course was relatively easy at first. But it built in its intensity and commitment.

When I looked at a different perspective on how I had eaten for three decades, I had my greatest insights as to how I had buried my life, my dreams, my plans, and vision, just by eating what I was used to.

At first, I struggled to connect the evidence with how I knew I degraded my body and rendered it dysfunctional. An Indian vegetarian diet was all I knew! I didn't know anything else!

Guess what? I wasn't alone. With the support of others who were all in a similar boat, we managed together, across continents and diets and cultures, to find a better way of eating.

Pretty quickly, the new seeds we planted and the old dreams we had long buried began to germinate. The reprogramming started to uncover the health and vitality that I had long covered with pain, illness, and dis-ease.

As we gained momentum, I realised that I had set my expectation bar too low. I just wanted to return to my so-called "ground zero" which was the time before my health degradation. But I quickly realized that I could do more because I *SURPASSED* my pre-ground-zero when we barely had completed MONTH ONE!

My body no longer reminded me that it needed medication!

Little did I realise at the time, but this single adjustment in health control shifted ALL other components of my life and created a whole new world. My slate was wiped clean. I went back to the body I had in my twenties in energy, stamina, look, and feel but kept with me the gift of hindsight.

I realized that I hadn't been buried. I had been planted and I was finally germinating, fresh as a daisy and bursting into bloom!

Impossible, but I'mPossible. Un-believable. And now that I've experienced it, I am no longer uncertain, terrified, or apprehensive about the future.

I know. I feel. And I wake up with healthy certainty. I have health certainty every single day.

I now have ongoing, boundless energy and stamina. I find myself making time for what's on my virtual-perpetual-to-do list! That list you just usually never get to.

I rest well. I sleep deeply. I create confidently. I passion-ise freely. I thrive delightedly. I celebrate thankfully. I am care FREE and at ease, more comfortable than I have ever been in my body and in my health status. I dropped three dress sizes in three months! Who wouldn't be ecstatic with all these upgrades?!?

Through this journey, I realised two things - that I wasn't buried and my dreams weren't obscured. I could dig up my vision and give it another go. In the past, I CONSCIOUSLY MADE that CHOICE to bury myself. And that choice was possible to REVISE.

During this reprogramming, I liberated my health and gave it status. It is now a measured part of my definition of success, a deliberate part of my retirement plan.

Because this challenge instilled habits that feel like they were always a part of me, my food choices and eating habits are now an unconscious part of every action I take.

I went from my body reminding me with pain and dysfunction that it was time to take medication to my body forgetting that it needed any crutches, patches, and bandages. I went from needing constant chiropractic care to no chiropractor in a YEAR and counting. And all this healing started within the space of a MONTH into reprogramming!

The reprogramming is so intense and so distinct; that if I opt to eat something that I used to consume regularly, my body reacts as if someone is plucking the one nerve that's strung tightly between my neck and my rear. And that's within minutes of consuming what I used to eat on a regular basis. It's no wonder I was single-handedly fast-tracking the payments on my chiropractor's retirement annuity!

Incredibly, PAIN has now become MY CHOICE. That's right. I have the choice of whether I want to be in pain and that decision is based on my eating habits!

Because of this reprogramming, I'm now on a mission to help people break free of stifling pre-burial habits, to help people live without the vision-limiting aches and pains that they believe is normal. I help people to reject the norm that disease and illness runs in families; and my deepest wish is to watch families germinate, blossom, and bloom in this new paradigm as they pursue their collective vision.

In short...

I help people to reprogram their health and vitality, to throw away outdated health paradigms, and to re-germinate the life vision they once buried under the yoke of pain, illness, and dis-ease. I also empower others to bloom in their pain-less, dis-ease-free life vision.

Through this, I am continually reminded of one constant:

Your health is your greatest wealth. Don't bury it first.

Vindina Mitha is a foodie-deluxe masquerading as the voice behind Soul Food, a health and wellness practice that helps people to rediscover their **food and life freedom** by reconstructing the fundamental narratives around what human beings cannot hide from – food. Soul Food has a decidedly different, decidedly simple, decidedly gentle, and decidedly efficient approach to health, vitality, and overall wellness by tying ancestral diets to the modern-day lifestyle and bringing the body and mind into cohesive balance.

Vindina believes that we are way too complacent in accepting chronic pain, daily medication, illness, and ways of life that support non-functional bodies and dis-ease. Having come through her own upgrade, shedding her pain dependencies, and eradicating her reliance on functional and top-up medication, Vindina knows that major lifestyle adoption is not easy. That's why her mission is to foster smooth transitions and to support those who *want to* fast-track their health and vitality to live pain and dis-ease-free.

Vindina unconditionally supports those who are willing to transform themselves and their families. She harnesses this enthusiasm together with her passion, knowledge, and nurturing nature to serve her clients unconditionally.

Vindina shows her clients how to break free of these self-imposed, self-limiting constraints. She loves getting her tribe to the point where they start reframing their lives to reincorporate the vision that they have in their heads and in their hearts, but which have, over time, become buried by all the degradation in their health. She thoroughly enjoys watching her tribe find their inner songs, dances, and re-enchantments though their unfolding transformations.

Vindina co-creates these full-body transformations by being instrumental in shifting her clients' health and by integrating and building habits that support health on a physical and mental level. In this way, she enables her clients to think less about their health so they will have more time and energy to devote to their loved ones and other parts of their lives. This methodology is how she helps her tribe to throw away any outdated notions they may have about their health potential.

As an avid foodie, Vindina adores creating and experimenting in the kitchen, which she believes is the heart and the hearth of the home. As an eager zero-waster, she continually looks for ways in which to practice mindfulness in consumption. She is always open to learning new methods of repurposing. Vindina is currently renovating her heritage home in Port Elizabeth, South Africa and enjoys finding ways in which to blend the old with the new.

If you want to find out more, Vindina has an active Facebook page where she shares content on both Instagram and Facebook @SoulFoodFreedom.

Vindina would love to see you engage with her, to learn, share, and grow together as a community. Contact her at https://www.facebook.com/SoulFoodFreedom if you are ready to upgrade to a pain-free, dis-ease-free life.

CHAPTER 5:

Supercalifragilistic-Expialidocious: A Word To Say When You Have No Words

By Alison Barbone

I'm outgoing but hate the spotlight. I think it is safe to say I'm more introvert than extrovert. Definitely happy in my own company. I mean, I can talk about anything but ask me to talk about myself, my journey, thoughts, or feelings and I suddenly feel very shy and get tongue-tied, embarrassed even. So why I ended up where I am now is still a bit of a mystery to me.

I always thought of myself as, not to put too fine of a point on it, just your average Mother of Boys. Nothing special or out of the ordinary.

But as I'm now finding out, I'm also so much more.

Let's turn the clock back 18 months:

I'm working three nights a week, one of which is a Sunday, and going to bed around 1 or 2am. I get up to do school runs as my husband leaves at 5am for work, then I run the house: shopping, laundry, occasional cleaning! You get the drift.

I am tired. Really tired. Already on mild antidepressants for anxiety as stress levels are insane at home with toddler number three, but that's a whole other story. I simply have no motivation. My days are spent in a sleepy haze, drinking gallons of coffee and Pepsi Max in an effort to give myself energy, going for fry-ups with the girls, and sitting on my backside watching television while playing Candy Crush. At least when I'm not falling asleep, that is.

It was a comfortable rut; don't get me wrong, I wasn't unhappy. I got to take the kids to school and pick them up every day, which a lot of working mums don't get to do. I missed out on that privilege with the first two.

I pretty much suited myself all day, every day.

However, that little Voice in the back of my head kept telling me I had to buck my ideas up. I knew my clothes were getting tighter, but I refused to go up another size. I had no energy, always snapping at the kids and my poor, hard-working husband.

I knew the Voice was right, I had to change. But before I knew it, another month passed and I'd still not made any positive steps to help myself feel better or quiet that Voice.

I'm not sure what triggered the big change, even now. There was no eureka moment or sign. I think it was a number of little circumstances that built up until I could no longer ignore them or the Voice.

The Big 4-0 was looming; I had a family wedding but refused to go up that dress size. I was fed up with being fed up, of feeling fat and bloated.

I reached out to a Facebook friend who I had followed for about a year and a half. I didn't know Carly personally and I think that helped; she could offer impartial advice with no judgement. Usually any requests from network marketers, especially in the weight-loss sector, were deleted and dismissed scathingly. But for some reason I'd kept Carly. I like to think now that the Universe knew I'd need her.

One message: Can you help me to lose weight?

Carly: Yes, what is your goal?

Me: Three stone would be amazing but just a stone off will spur me on.

Carly: That's definitely achievable. Our 'Love Your Body' plan, supported by the Juice Plus products is a lifestyle change, so the program teaches you to eat better and gives lasting results. Tell me about your current habits.

Me: Night work plays havoc with eating. Meals are not too bad but snacking is terrible. Sometimes don't even eat.

Carly: Okay, so you're skipping meals. This program will help you to eat better and not skip meals. How would you feel if you lost the weight?

Me: I'd feel bloody amazing. Just want to be fit again.

After a few more messages back and forth, I signed up to the top package. No point in doing things by half as usual! I was so determined to make this plan work, especially since I'd seen other client results. A huge weight lifted off me just making the decision to sign up to the program!

The plan came with a detox so I jumped straight in. I cut out coffee, Pepsi Max, bread, artificial sweeteners, gluten, and cheese. I found the change was so easy; I was definitely ready to kick all my bad habits. I even lost a few pounds the week I detoxed. That weight loss spurred me on to keep going.

Then products arrived. Whole-food supplements, vegan protein shakes, and fat-burning boosters. Within weeks I was feeling so much better, not nearly as tired. In two months, I'd lost nearly all the weight, two stone, and no longer napped during the day. I even got comments from my friends and family saying how well I looked. By holiday, I was confident enough to wear my bikini!

I honestly hadn't felt so good about myself in years.

You would think losing weight and feeling amazing and confident again was the end of my story, but no. There was even more to come. Something that I would never have pictured myself doing in a million years. In fact, had you told me the path I would end up going down, I would have laughed in your face.

Once I'd been on the products a few weeks, Carly asked me if I wanted to know about the business side of the program. "Don't be so ridiculous," I thought and politely declined. I had my job to earn money; I had no time to do anything else.

Then I responded to her Facebook post asking, "Who spends too much time on social media?" Definitely me! She replied, "If you spend time on social media, you should try the biz!"

I just laughed. I was afraid of the unknown and of being one of those annoying online-sales people. I didn't want to be somebody who bored their family and friends with constant nagging to join their group or use their products, no matter how incredible they were. "And who on earth would buy from me anyway?" I thought.

The next morning, I walked my eldest to school, discussing his upcoming football trip. The outing was a residential with kids he didn't know very well, but it was going to be a great experience and a chance to get to know the boys he attends Norwich Player Development Centre with once a week. We already paid for the trip and told him he was going. He wanted to go but was fearful that he did not know the boys well and was basically going alone. I said to him, "It's good to push yourself and do things outside of your comfort zone. Those opportunities make you a better person."

BOOM. The penny dropped. Who was I to tell him to challenge himself when I myself was refusing an opportunity that literally landed in my lap?

I messaged Carly, "Go on and tell me all about the Juice Plus business opportunity then. It won't hurt to see what is involved." Immediately, I felt quite sick but excited, which was a bit odd! It was only a meeting after all, but I felt sick with excitement and nerves about where it could lead. Taking this step was so far out of my comfort zone, what was I doing?

The day we met, I was nervous since the meeting almost felt like a job interview, but also calm, like somehow, I knew all would be okay. Carly was so easy to talk to so we chatted for ages over a coffee. She explained a bit more how the business works and what I needed to do in order to get involved. She herself had been in my position, started by using the products then signed up to the business. She talked to me about her own experience and what the business had done for her. No pressure, no big income claims, just honest chat. And it felt like we'd known each other forever.

I agreed there and then to sign up! The sign-up fee was hardly anything and if I did well, I'd make it back my first month. I figured that if I made enough to cover my product cost every month, I'd be on to a really good idea.

I always sat around on my phone, after all, and the entire business model hinged on using social media, as well as old-fashioned word of mouth, to gain interest.

As with everything I start, I jumped in both feet first and ran with it. I didn't have a clue as to what I was doing but knew I would figure it out as I went along. The Company literally does most of the work for its franchise partners: shipping, payments, stock holding. All I had to do was to share the incredible products and business opportunity on my social media. I also got to share my own story and finally process orders. Simple.

I hit my first promotion within a month and in two months I hit the next one. I couldn't believe it! I actually covered the cost of my products and made some extra cash on top.

That's when I started to see the bigger picture. This style of working was something that I was actually quite good at. I enjoyed the work, helped others, and had the potential to achieve the dream of quitting my night job.

So, I threw myself into the work even more. More social media content, more customer care, more connections, more everything!

It's hard working online at times. You just sit on your phone, connecting and chatting with like- minded people from all over the World and you get a lot of resistance from people that think Network Marketing isn't a proper job. Well no, it isn't. And thank goodness for that! I've done my days of the 9-to-5 grind for mediocre money. I've sacrificed my family time. If there's a way *around* that drudgery then I'll keep going, thanks all the same!

I went to my company's convention in Brighton and it blew me away. To be in a room surrounded by all those like-minded people, wanting to build a better, brighter future for themselves, while helping others to do the same. Absolutely. Incredible. The convention really reaffirmed why I wanted to sign up and become a part of this amazing Juice Plus family in the first place.

I have dropped my shifts at Tesco down to two a week and no longer have to do lots of overtime to earn extra income. Just the extra time at home alone has made such a big difference to our family life. Our weekends are now ours again. No clock-watching, waiting until I have to go in on a Sunday night. As much as I enjoy my little job at night, I know once my business is fully grown and operating successfully, I will be able to leave Tesco behind and become fully self-employed. I don't have to; many people fly high within Juice Plus alongside full and part-time jobs, but that's not for me. That's not my goal.

People do this business for many reasons and like I said, my decision to join in was initially just to cover my products. But now, now I want to take this journey as far as I can. I want to bring more income to the table, relieve my husband of the sole-breadwinner pressure. Yes, I could go find a 'real job' but that would inevitably mean paying for childcare and sacrificing even more family time. Online work with Juice Plus also has far more earning potential than any part-time job for a working mum. It takes time to build up the clientele and team, just like any 'real' business, but the possibility is there.

This business has dared me to dream bigger, to believe in myself more (although that is a work in progress), to get in touch with my spiritual side again, to learn gratitude and practice it, and to just try and be the best version of myself. The version that inadvertently got buried since getting married and having children. I don't think you realise that you can lose yourself as a mother; you just have other interests and challenges that became more important. I think the danger is that we're so busy looking after everyone else's needs, we put ourselves to the back of the queue, without even realising it.

I often wish I had known about the Juice Plus products and business opportunity after having my first son. It's not that Juice Plus wasn't around, it was. I guess I just wasn't open to seeing or hearing about the benefits or opportunity. I like to think I saw the light as it was, when I was ready and open to learn. I'm on the right path now and that's all that matters.

My main aim now is to build a big movement of my own, retire the husband, save for three-boys'-worth of first cars, weddings, houses, and dare I say it, grandchildren. To give them all the help I can and show them that anything is possible if you truly believe.

As for me and my husband, we want to travel more and have a holiday apartment in the Canaries. We have often talked about offering emergency foster care, owning self-catering holiday lets, or opening an Italian deli. And now, all of those choices are actually possible.

The future is so much brighter with the backing of this amazing business. I used to say my only legacy was providing three more well-raised humans for the planet. But now, I have a chance to make a real difference, not only to my life but to countless other women's as well.

I'm still learning as I go and won't ever stop because that's when my business will stop growing.

At 41, I'm fitter, healthier, happier, and more in love with Life than ever and cannot wait to see where this journey takes me next.

Because of this amazing turn in own my life, I'm now able to coach you in how to make the changes you have put off and help you put yourself first again. With the incredible whole-food Juice Plus products and our Love Your Body Plan I can help you with your health, weight, and confidence. There is an amazing exclusive client-support group on Facebook, where I will give you all the one-on-one mentoring you want. There are also weekly meal plans and even exercise guides to keep you on track and feeling good.

With the available franchise opportunities, I can help you regain control of your finances without sacrificing your family time. You can have more of a social life and even travel if you wish to. You earn commission on every order you place, including your own. You will be given your own website and a virtual office on sign-up. What other business can give you that much for only £50?

As cheesy as sounds, starting Juice Plus really did change my life. It was the support I needed when I couldn't make the changes I wanted to make by myself. Now, I'm able to be your support and that is truly an honour.

Alison Barbone, Ali to her friends, is your average 41-year-old, blue eyed, left-handed, Doc Marten-wearing, Harry Potter-loving, self-confessed telly addict, foodie, and mother of boys.

Originally North London born and bred, she now lives in St. Neots, Cambridgeshire, with her husband of 13 years Felice, their three sons, Thomas, Vincenzo, and Santino, and the family cat Apollo.

Alison worked since she was 13-years old, starting out in the local grocery shop. After A Levels she chose to work instead of going down the University route. After having her third child, she decided to stay at home since the commute to London and childcare costs were more than her wage.

Three years later, she went back to her retail roots, working at Tesco two nights a week to fit around the children while helping make ends meet. This job began to take its toll after increasing to three nights a week, while Alison still juggled the ever-increasing demands of her family and home.

That is when an opportunity landed in her lap and she became, much to her surprise, a business woman. She now works for Juice Plus, a Health and Wellness Franchise, helping other tired mums to get back on their feet and find themselves again, just as she herself accomplished with great success. With incredible whole-food supplements to boost body, mind, and energy and encouragement to follow a nutrition plan, Alison supports other women to achieve their health goals and design a new life for them and their families.

If you want to find out more, she can be found on Facebook and Facebook Messenger at:
www.facebook.com/alison.barbone.5

Or on her website at www.alisonbarbone.juiceplus.com

She would love to have a chat with you today. There is never any pressure, so just take a deep breath and enquire. What have you got to lose? And more to the point, what could you *gain*?

CHAPTER 6:

Let Love Find You

By Agnieszka Burban

Despite fitting the description of a "perfect girl" for most of my life, I was deeply unhappy in love.

Looking back at my love life, the time I spent with the men I loved most was turbulent, full of anxiety, disconnection, and loneliness.

Take, for instance, my relationship with D.

We met when I was in my 20s and fell in love almost immediately. But the red flags started early on. D spent most of his time in pubs with his buddies. I felt confused and disappointed. I never knew when he would be back home.

As time went by, our relationship was governed by emotional turbulence. We grew further apart. I became emotionally starved and felt very lonely. I went through periods of deep anxiety and low mood swings which were often combined with a spell of poor health. For several years I struggled with my health and energy, unintentionally losing a lot of weight.

D was not supportive.

One day while at our friends' wedding, I had an anxiety attack and had to walk to a nearby park to calm down. I asked D to stay with me for a while. After only five minutes, he returned to the wedding, leaving me all alone. I walked down the park path by myself, crying and thinking, "Am I really not worth 20 minutes of his attention?"

I desperately craved being held and touched to feel a connection. When we moved to London, I often watched couples hug and kiss while I waited on the platform for the tube to arrive. This physical contact was exactly what I wanted so much! I felt deeply sad and jealous watching those couples.

My instincts whispered to me that love was more than anxiety and a deep thirst for connection. I craved being really wanted, cherished, and loved. One day, my engagement ring snapped whilst I was washing my hands. I looked at it, took it off, and thought to myself: "Wow, this broken ring is just like our relationship…"

D and I eventually broke up after 13 years of being together. The ending was not as difficult as I thought it would be since the relationship felt 'dead' already. We both felt it was time to move on, going our separate ways.

And so, I embarked on a self-discovery journey.

A few months after the breakup with D, I mustered courage and downloaded a dating app. However, the men I met were not emotionally available. Essentially, none of these men were willing to put me first in their lives.

So, I decided to focus on completing my psychotherapy studies and developing deep connections with my friends. Inspired by one of my housemates' travel stories, I decided to go on holiday to the 'hippie,' green La Gomera. My first solo trip. A new experience I felt truly excited about.

On my second day in La Gomera, I saw a man who became my soulmate a mere six weeks later. Since he lived in Sweden, we first stayed in touch as friends via text messages. But we both felt there was more than friendship in the air. This connection became clear when he visited me in London six weeks after our first encounter.

For one whole year, we flew between our two countries every few weeks. We also exchanged countless messages daily and often spoke on Skype.

On a few occasions I made shorts trips to Sweden to meet his children and his family. Every moment together seemed to move us towards a "happy ending." We felt a deep sense of connection with each other and awaited the day we could live together.

Eventually, I said goodbye to my friends and moved to Sweden. I had no idea how I would make a home in a new country without knowing anybody there apart from my boyfriend and his family. Not to mention how I would cope financially, having only a few clients at the time.

However, I deeply believed that if we really loved each other so much, we would overcome any obstacles. "Love conquers all," I strongly believed.

Deep down, I knew that the house he lived in did not meet my needs. I turned a blind eye to this fact, believing that our love could help me overcome my concerns. The walls were thin and all of the ground-floor level was an "open space" design which made the sound travel upstairs easily.

The house was a sound nightmare to my sensitive brain!

As a result, I became increasingly more anxious. I returned home each evening, dreading the invasion of all the sounds. The anticipation caused me to nearly have a panic attack, even before I stepped through the door.

Soon enough, I got very ill. I was so stressed and anxious, that I suffered a severe mental breakdown! And this anxiety was just too much for my boyfriend. My state triggered a stress reaction in him so he was not able to be there for me when I needed him most.

In a way, this was a repeat of the situation with D. I was just "too much" and a "burden" to those I loved.

Not long after that, he asked me to sit on the sofa to "talk." I knew what he wanted to say. I felt unwanted and discarded. I felt betrayed.

But there was far more I had to face than the breakdown of our relationship. I was ill, depressed, and suddenly I had no home and very meagre funds to support myself.

There I was, in a foreign country with hardly any friends, and I had no idea how to resolve the housing issue I faced. The most logical decision was to return to where I came from; buy a ticket to London, find another office-based job, rent a room somewhere.

But deep down, there was a strong intuition inside me saying what seemed completely unreasonable, "Stay in Sweden!" So, I listened to that voice and stayed.

I found a flat which became my small safety nest. I could not really afford it, as my salary at the time barely covered the rent, but I trusted that solutions would somehow come at the right time.

I often visited my friends in London who provided a sense of comfort and support while I made a new way in Sweden.

During one of my visits to London, I found out that the renowned author and relationship expert, Katherine Woodward Thomas, was giving a workshop about conscious uncoupling. I felt an instinctive urge to attend it.

Katherine's talk felt like a balm on my soul; she talked about how to process the pain of a breakup in a way which propelled it into something meaningful. She spoke about relationships, love, and how we are called and destined to have the relationship we want, which instilled new hope in me. At last I could see a crack of light at the end of the tunnel.

Katherine also mentioned becoming one of her "Calling in 'The One'" coaches, which involved personal mentoring from Katherine, to be trained in her unique method and invite healthy, happy love. Again, my intuition told me that I needed to do this training. It was something I wanted to do for myself, but I also felt the desire to help other women who, like me, struggled to find fulfilling and lasting love.

This training allowed me to embark on an entirely new journey, to learn all I needed about myself, relationships, and love. I started a whole new chapter in my life.

A few weeks after the London workshop, I began the training, spending many evenings listening to long calls, but also undergoing my own Calling in 'The One' coaching process, a method all of Katherine's trainees had to go through.

During that training process, I began to change.

I experienced what Katherine referred to as a change of "love identity." I processed the breakdown of the relationship with my ex-boyfriend and started to see myself and my past experiences in a new light.

From this new perspective, I was no longer a suffering victim. In fact, I was a victor!

I felt strong, empowered, and I understood that if I had not been through all the previous turmoil and suffering, I would not have grown.

I understood that my ex-boyfriend and his ability to meet my needs was simply a reflection of my own ability to meet my needs. After all, at the beginning of our story, I chose not to focus on my worries around the noise issues in his house. By accepting that discomfort, I chose to turn a blind eye to one of my basic needs.

Throughout my own Calling in 'The One' journey, I had to challenge several of my old, limiting, and unhealthy beliefs about myself and love; I began to foster new, healthy beliefs instead. I cleared all the toxic bonds and relationships in my life, both past and present.

As I went through the process, I gained the unwavering certainty that my dream man would one day cross my path.

Immediately after I completed my training, my very first client Doreen, a 50-year old woman with a long track record of failed relationships, found the most beautiful, loving, and committed man. She successfully broke her old relationship patterns after merely eight weeks of coaching with me.

I knew that the teaching I received worked, but to *see* it transform someone's life, in such a short time, was a completely different dimension.

As for me, my soul partner crossed my path a few weeks later. At the time, I was dating a man who showed many traits of my ex-dates and ex-lovers. But I was not the same woman as before. I knew what I wanted. So, I thanked my date for the time we spent together and said I did not wish to date him anymore. He didn't take my message on board, so he continued to contact me. In the end, I felt I had no choice but to block his number.

I call this particular technique "Closing the Door." Sometimes we need to do or say whatever it takes to stop interacting with someone who is not aligned with our vision of a relationship.

Straight after I closed the door on that ill-matched relationship, I received a message from my current soul partner Johannes!

What was extraordinary about the way he came into my life was that the process was easy. I did not have to date hundreds of men online to find 'The One.' Yes, I had two dating experiences with men who were not my "match" before I met the right man, but I could use the tools from my training to "decode" what I needed from these encounters to be even more ready to welcome the right man.

What is different now? Everything.

To start off, I feel safe in my relationship. I can *relax* in it without a fear that my man will surprise me with an emotional withdrawal or start blaming me for various situations or circumstances. I no longer experience anxiety in love. I feel calm, wanted, and prioritised.

You see, once we change our belief system about ourselves and what we can have in love, we make different choices. We should never choose what is not aligned with our highest good. And once that transformation is in place, we start attracting people who reflect what we deeply believe in.

I cannot resist sharing one extraordinary fact about this process that happened to me as well: often we get even more than what we had expected!

Do you remember how I struggled with the "noise issue" and the role it played in the breakup of my previous relationship? Since I did not recognise my need for a quiet space was a legitimate, basic need of mine, my ex-partner mirrored this belief back to me by not being able to meet my needs. He did offer to convert the small shed in the garden into an office for me at one point. But when it turned out to be more difficult than imagined, he abandoned the project.

I never mentioned any part of this story to my current partner. A few weeks into our relationship, he took me on a hike and when we got tired, we stopped for some tea. I shared with him my dream to have a space where I could work away from home. And then he said:

"There is a space in the garden which I wanted to convert into an exercise room. But I can easily convert it into an office for you!"

The look on his face told me, "Yeah, it is not a big deal."

"Are you serious?" I asked in a timid voice.

"Yes, it is not a problem at all," he said.

And he kept his word.

In fact, many aspects of my former relationship struggles took a complete 180° turn. My current partner fully supports me with my paperwork. Without him I would have never paved my way through the Swedish tax system. He has a 100%-unwavering belief in my business and my mission.

When I have a bad day or feel sad, he is right there, ready to hug me and comfort me. I am finally … *seen*. My needs are acknowledged and met. And I am fully supported.

Once you change your love identity and you welcome your soul partner into your life, areas that used to feel like a struggle in your relationships are no longer an issue. I do not worry about the future and you don't have to either.

The life I have is simply a reflection of what I think is possible and my partner is a reflection of how I love and care for myself, how kind I am to myself, and how much I am able to listen to my own feelings.

As I write these words, I can see the face of one of my clients, Gill, who recently sent me a picture in which her partner lovingly kisses her on the cheek. They look so madly happy and care-free. A few weeks ago, this very same woman was emotionally involved with another man who told her he was not ready to be in a relationship with her. Now, those days are a distant memory for her. She has attracted a man who wants to be and *is* fully committed to her. They even jokingly talk about marriage! That is a huge change from the very same woman who told me at the beginning of our work together "*I will never marry again!*"

Gill no longer attracts emotionally unavailable men nor is she interested in them. She sets clear, healthy boundaries with others, and for the first time, she is able to trust enough to be vulnerable with a man and express her true feelings. In other words, *she* herself has become *available* to be loved. And she attracted an emotionally and physically available man who fully reflects her true self. Someone who is caring, generous, and ready to put her first.

If you are curious to find out more about how to welcome this kind of love into your life, I would like to invite you to watch my mini training, "3 Steps to Let Love Find You." I explain in three short videos the crucial steps you need to take in order to allow love into your life in an easy and anxiety-free way.

To access the training, go to: http://bit.ly/let-love-find-you

To Your Happy Love Life,

Agnieszka

Agnieszka Burban is The Lasting Love Expert for single women over 30. She was trained by the renowned psychotherapist and relationship expert Katherine Woodward Thomas, the author of the national bestselling book, *Calling in "The One."*

She is also a licensed and practising psychotherapist, trained at the prestigious Institute of Psychology, Psychiatry, and Neuroscience in London, a world-leading research and training centre. She has published articles on relationship psychology and dating with Welldoing.org, the UK's leading therapist-matching service.

Her clients are single women over 30 who are accomplished and successful but have one thing missing from their lives -- a fulfilling romantic relationship. Women who work with Agnieszka have experienced great emotional pain in their previous relationships and yearn for a lasting relationship that makes them feel safe and secure. Her mission is to help thousands of women overcome the barriers to love and to help them cherish relationships so they feel loved, nurtured, and safe.

Agnieszka first made a breakthrough in her own love life in her 40s, using the very system she teaches others through her coaching programme and in her online communities. She now cherishes a happy, healthy relationship characterised by safety, sweetness, and trust. Her teachings and programme comprise cutting-edge relationship psychology with a unique energy system designed for those who want to experience a radical breakthrough in their love life.

Agnieszka is free-spirited, creative, and fun-loving. She adores spending time by lakes and woods as well as the endless cups of tea she cannot live without. She lives in Sweden with her beloved partner.

If you are tired of attracting men who are emotionally unavailable, not willing to commit, or simply the wrong type of men, and you are ready to call in "The One," and finally feel loved and cherished the way you have always wanted, click here to download Agnieszka´s mini training "*3 Steps to Let Love Find You*", where she will explain in 3 short videos the crucial steps you need to take to allow love into your life in an easy, clear, and anxiety-free way. To access the training go to:

http://bit.ly/let-love-find-you

CHAPTER 7:

Unstoppable

By Małgorzata Biernacka

Business expansion did not come to me at night in a dream or as an idea during sleepless nights. It came to me in the ICU while I waited for my 80-year-old father to wake up after his cancer surgery. I waited for two weeks, every day, but unfortunately, he never woke up. His spirit decided to stay wherever he was during his operation.

The last time I saw him in the hospital, a night before the surgery, was the last time my parents hugged me together. They decided to protect me, not sharing the true nature of my father's surgery. I discovered the severity of the procedure only during his admission to the hospital. I was not given the time to absorb the shock. I tried to hold up all the fear and tears, but I failed and cried, unable to give him proper encouragement or cheer him up a little in his misery. I could not focus on anything else but crossing my fingers, hoping for my father to survive his operation, and supporting my mother.

Unfortunately, the matters took a deadly course. My father grew weaker and weaker. During his time in the ICU, he went through two other operations that were supposed to fix the first one. But after two long weeks when he was neither here nor there, he gave up and passed away. My mother and I were devastated. I could not work for the next several weeks and only started to truly function again after a few months.

My consulting business and clients were immediately put on hold. I realized that I needed to shift my focus to support my mother and prepare our family for what was supposed to come next. During that hard time, I realized the need for a location-free and time-independent business so I could continue to work while taking care of family matters.

Maggie's Hub – a 100% online coaching business which supports consultants, coaches and other kick-ass experts ready to move their offline business online – was a result of that very first thought. But this concept was not born as an easy, straightforward answer to my online-business calling. It took me a good 12 months to arrive at its actual, final shape and feel comfortable in my new role. This journey was far from easy and even further from being simple. Despite the fact I was well trained, a professional marketer with extensive experience in a variety of markets, I still had to learn a million tasks, one after another, in a short time. It was both frustrating and energy draining, but I learned so much along the way.

I started from the worst possible angle: developing my website. I had rich experience with webs, even award-winning ones! But I had never produced one myself, with my own hands! That was a totally different game, ladies and gentlemen! To this day, I have no idea what devil whispered into my ear, "You can do it; building a website is deadly easy! Why don't you just learn how to produce a website in WordPress, the most popular platform these days, and establish it yourself from A to Z? You can even learn a bit of coding. It will be so precious…"

You know what? Creating the site was relatively uncomplicated, but it was so very time-consuming. I worked on that website for almost six months, and during that time I did not even have time to reflect back on any other concerns. Instead, I kept myself so busy with this project, I literally had no time for anything else! I believed my website needed to be complete from the very start. People would be looking!

I thought my website needed to contain EVERYTHING, including blog posts, podcasts and videos, SEO and backlinks, and God knows what else! I benchmarked myself with top online-business consultants in the US. I did not realize how high I positioned this bar for myself. On the conscious level, I was fully aware that online businesses I admired were built over many years. But somehow, on my subconscious level, I was sure I needed to launch my business from that same, unachievable level. As a result, I turned myself into a writer, graphic designer, podcast and video producer, editor, and senior multi-tasker. I stood firmly with the opinion that MY website was required to be professional. Otherwise, I would not be perceived as competent by my clients, my colleagues, my friends, or my family. So, I put myself on the track that led me towards significant mistakes and the enormous consequences which had a colossal impact on my business.

My focus was 100% on my website, not my business, not my clients, not my offer! Funny enough, my website contained EVERYTHING but my sales offer. Honestly, I could not figure out exactly what I would sell online! And this indecisiveness happened because I was guilty of yet another mistake typical for so many entrepreneurs – I procrastinated. Big time! The web project created for me the full spectrum of alibis to cover the fact I was not selling any of my services.

However, thanks to this experience, I discovered one of the biggest and most common mistakes that new online entrepreneurs make. Developing a website in a smooth way requires solid preparations, competences in online communication, digital marketing, decisions related to the online brand positioning, and crystal clarity in the area of the sales offer. Not to mention the technical and technological stuff like domains, URLs, web platforms, plug-ins, coding, SEO etc. They all create subject matters that are unrecognizable in full spectrum to first-time online entrepreneurs. These processes are not easy, even for experienced business owners or marketers like myself.

After several months of trying, I sadly came to the conclusion that initiating online existence through web creation simply contributes to a massive energy loss and causes excessive stress levels and huge frustrations to build up at the same time. Understanding this phenomenon allowed me create a coaching program which allows offline businesses to gain an online presence without the website, while still gaining clients successfully. I will always remain deeply grateful for that lesson no matter how hard it was to learn.

But before the enlightening moment occurred to me, I stayed busy with everything that seemed far more critical at the time. Selling was never my strong point, and I avoided it like the plague whenever I could. In my mind, selling was a bit dirty, slightly pushy, and definitely nothing for me! I never needed to generate sales proactively at any time before. Consulting clients came through recommendations and always provided enough business for me. I was really good at strategy, managing the most complicated projects, sometimes with the most challenging people. Yet, I believed I could not sell. So, I did not.

Instead, I firmly believed that I needed to improve my online skills, to quickly become a web-design expert on the world-class level! So, I started to buy and read through courses that were supposed to help me with my website content creation. I confidently put my eyes on classes for video production, how to look good for the camera, how to create an e-course, and about a dozen similar projects. None of them was about selling with confidence or starting my first business steps online! None about procrastination, none about making a revolution in life, none about getting shit done!

On some level, I was perfectly aware of what was happening. My rational inner voice tried to point out the misery of my actions. But my ego shouted stronger and louder, succeeding to add new things onto my to-do list. I didn't realize the internal voice was actually my ego until some weeks later, but at the time I was sure I needed to follow this command inside me. I recognized it as my rational voice, directing me towards a happy ending, all while explaining the importance of completing that bloody to-do list.

The days passed by, one after another, but I could not see the end of my actions. I became a slave to my own project and the slave of time. There was never enough time, although I gave my project full priority. I engaged in my work for 10 to 12 hours daily, not having time for anything else. I set up my environment to serve my cause. EVERYBODY knew I was opening Maggie's Hub - my new project. My family and friends were really understanding and supportive. But at one point, I realized that I had lost eight kilos and felt tired, sweaty, and irritated all the time. I turned into a zombie! I have to admit, this process was not exactly how I envisaged the online business expansion! I was exhausted, far from launching, but definitely not ready to drop my dream.

I felt so exhausted, I decided finally to visit a doctor and get a full medical diagnosis to determine what was wrong with me. They ran series of lab tests and diagnostics in the hospital as I heard them mention a strange name – Grave's disease. The diagnosis was an auto-immune disorder resulting in a massive thyroid imbalance. When the doctor saw my lab tests, he was surprised I was still conscious because such low results should have triggered a coma. Auto-immune diseases like Grave's or Hashimoto's often form as a result of long-term stress or a series of devastating events. At that time, I was unaware of the negative stresses happening around me. I had supportive, loving family, a great husband ready to help at any moment, and a pleasant, balanced life – at first glance, zero stress factors. Yet there was one little problem still. My mindset was severely imbalanced.

Every day for the previous months, I had faced all kinds of self-doubts, insecurities, fears, and uncertainties. I felt devastated and lost. I questioned my ability to express my thoughts clearly, how to word each post, the type of content I decided to offer my audience. I could not find the way out of the mess or take time to honour any of my fears. Likewise, I could not accept the situation as it was.

I did not know at the time that my insecurities were the result of so called "ego talk." Ego, in reality, is our conditioned mind whose sole role is to keep the status quo, making sure we do not use too much of the energy that might be necessary for survival. Most of our fears and insecurities are the ego's strategy to discourage us and direct us back to the previous, safe, old situation. I was completely unaware, like most people, that if I recognised the fears and addressed them, I could convert them into my power. I could confront the ego consciously and make some long-expected progress while facing my fears.

I had allowed my ego to whip me all over for months, making sure all my imperfections, and self-doubts were well-planted in my head. My ego did its job so well that I finally started to believe that my knowledge, experience, language, and genuine personality were not good enough for the mission I had the ambition to accomplish. I perceived myself as small and almost defeated. Half-human. Not worth it.

The first seeds that caused my auto-immune disease reached a very fertile ground of stress and anxiety. Today, I understand how the aggressive development of my disease was even possible. I, the fighter who reformulated my life from ground zero several times, kept thinking "I am not good enough, my English sucks, I cannot express my thoughts clearly, people will not listen, nobody will buy anything from me." Despite the fact that I felt physically unhealthy and emotionally miserable, every morning I pushed myself to work on my project. Even though my disease did not allow me to concentrate fully for more than twenty to thirty minutes I kept working in smaller time slots. Yet, I did not feel any closer to finalizing my project. On the contrary - my to-do list grew longer every day!

At some point, I realized that I spun my efforts for nothing. I could continue to entirely fulfil the wishes of my ego, but I became aware that it would not bring me any closer to my dream. I was not ready to stop and unwilling to drop the idea of Maggie's Hub. I genuinely wanted to support female entrepreneurs around the globe. Yet, I remained overworked, drained, and exhausted.

I needed a breakthrough. A direction. A turning point. One decision.

Finally, I committed to change my course of actions for good. My first decision that, "Enough is enough!" created the foundation for my future progress. All other decisions that followed after the first one formulated my survival strategy. For the moment, it did not look like a real, solid strategy, but rather a selection of steps to help secure my progress in the project, while at the same time dealing with all my insecurities and ego talk.

Step One – Decide who is in charge

I was aware that my priority was to keep the new status quo: I was in charge, not my fears or insecurities. To support myself quickly and load my batteries with the new energy I turned to my "secret resilience resource." This combination of my genuine personality features had almost been buried by my ego talk while I worked hard on the project and at the time my disease appeared.

The first advantages I drew on were a positive approach towards challenges and endless optimism - the qualities my parents implanted during my early childhood. Over time, I backed that approach up with exceptional gratitude. I learned mindfully to notice and acknowledge the smallest gifts around me, such as a sunny day, a nice cup of tea, or young plants in the spring. I reminded myself to start each day acknowledging that I am in charge, not my fears.

In order to recognize all my accomplishments, I created a list honouring all the skills and competences I acquired. Whenever I felt down and started to hear little voice of the ego trying to talk me out of the project, I looked at the list of accomplishments. This small practice supported me big-time during my toughest moments of self-doubt.

Step Two – If needed, burn the bridges

I was determined to support my project like a lioness. I craved to start and to launch Maggie's Hub on the market. However, with the long list of to-dos the deadline was pushed several times. I planned to launch in December, then in February, April. Eventually, I burned the bridges and set up a point of no return. I agreed with myself on a deadline for the official launch, a non-negotiable date in May, 2019. I was scared to death and not entirely sure how this decision would work. Would I stand firmly behind this date or postpone like I did several times before? In the long run, I was able to face my fears. This choice created one of the pillars of my quick progress.

Step Three – Confront your self-talk, address the ego

My ego went insane. The list of new tasks that seemed absolutely necessary before the launch and the number of fears I had to face got longer and scarier every day. I knew I had to stop my ego immediately and for good. From the depth of my heart, I heard this message: "Send the jerk away. Far away." Unfortunately, the only procedure I knew from my coaching training was to shut the ego down, a severe technique that feels like facing the dragon or devil or huge spider — whatever scares you to death. Nonetheless I was ready to give it a try.

Where and how I could send my ego away was still a mystery for me, but a plan started to form. I waited patiently, knowing that very soon I would get more information. And then one morning, I suddenly received in my head the very clear picture of a beautiful island, one with white sand, a blue, crystal-clear ocean all around, fantastic greenery, and comfortable sofas on the beach. That was a perfect place for my ego; I did not want to harm it and anticipated that perhaps one day I would be ready to be re-united with it again.

The plan to set aside my ego was ready and I decided to execute it same afternoon. I was no longer scared at all. I sat comfortably in my beloved armchair as I quieted my mind and my breath with eyes closed. It was like a meditation. I envisaged taking my ego on a walk into the forest. Simply and quietly, like I walk my dogs out in nature. My ego did not take any form or shape so it felt like walking together, but somehow separately.

I explained how grateful I was for all the work it made me accomplish over last months; for the protection, for directing my focus to the critical areas, for the additional abilities I learned. I thanked my ego profusely. I hugged it vigorously even though it did not have any form or shape, and I let it go. The ego argued, negotiated, and tried to take over again. But I was stronger this time and fully aware of what was happening.

With all my power, I simply said to my ego: "My love, you are going on a trip. The next weeks, perhaps months, you will spend on this beautiful island, and you will rest. You need time to recharge; poor thing, you look exhausted! You have done a great job, but now you feel drained. You will stay on the island and I will take care of our stuff. Off you go! Shoo!" I listened for a while but in the silence, it seemed the ego really disappeared.

I have learned how to face the ego, confront it, negotiate with it, and manage it all while transforming my fears into unstoppable power. Because I am stronger, we exist again together, but I am always in charge. My ego's job now is simply to point out the areas that require my special focus.

Step Four – Start selling immediately

Since I did not offer my services for over a year, I was determined to connect with a coach who could teach me effortless and confident ways of creating sales conversations and transforming them into happy, paying clients. I dreamed that the process was easy, saving me the struggle. As a sensitive introvert, I believed that I simply suck at selling but I felt determined to change that perception.

There is a saying, "When the student is ready, the teacher will appear." Mine materialized within two weeks of my decision to pursue a coach and taught me the mastery of energetic sales and marketing, the most effortless method of selling on the planet. This type of sales is always aligned with your dreams and your personality. It combines the best sales and marketing strategies and tactics that attract clients with ease, create powerful visibility online, claim expert positioning, and address the challenges of accelerated growth. I love it! This new method of merging the strategic work with energetic and spiritual elements allows me to fast-track my clients, taking their offline businesses online, so they acquire new clients much faster and enjoy extraordinary growth.

Step Five – Mindset, authenticity, and simplicity

The minute I started acquiring new clients and worked on their online business expansion, I realized how frequently women subconsciously add to the complexity of their life by unnecessary pessimism, scarcity, ruminating, and self-doubts. They behave exactly like I did when I was building my website. Strong, fantastic female entrepreneurs who have already set up at least one offline business often feel alone, powerless, confused, and full of fears. They believe that their online presence must be better than who they are offline. Perhaps stronger, more confident, more impressive.

The lesson I discovered during my online journey and the one I always share with my clients is, "Present yourself as authentically as possible, using your genuine personality and your own know-how. You are ready the way you are. You do not need to be "more" of anything: more confident, more international or more American, more professional, more fun. You do not need to be more. You are enough!" At first they cannot believe this advice is true but when they fully grasp the idea of authenticity and show their true personality, the magic happens. Clients relate to the authentic human beings, not actors or pretenders.

I am not a fan of checklists or long preparations anymore. That was a tremendous shift of my mindset. I always believed in preparation and old-school hard work. However, since I learned a simpler method, I run my business on-the-go. I do not prepare any articles, posts, courses, videos, or any other materials before they are really needed. This approach required some discipline to NOT complete tasks in advance. But I have to admit, the method pays me back by giving me extra time every day. I have learned to listen to my intuition during my morning meditation. During this 20 to 30-minute practice I work on my mindset and usually receive the guidance on the action steps to communicate best with my future clients, to acquire new clients, or to prepare new programs. I do not need to build complicated funnels or multi-element marketing campaigns. I concentrate daily on one to three tasks that I have to accomplish. No more long to-do lists!

These steps not only helped me complete my first launch on time but contributed to my first €14K-month only three months later. Since then, I have developed several programs to help my clients - female coaches, consultants, and kick-ass experts – to fast track their visibility and claim their expert position online. With ease. No complicated funnels needed!

My *Become Visible, Fearless and Unstoppable* programs combine the strategic and marketing side of business with spiritual and energetic work. This unique combination of the best business strategies and tactics, backed up with the most powerful mindset practices and a pinch of tech magic, allow every business owner to expand and accelerate their growth while confidently facing the self-doubts and fears that happen on the way.

Should you feel inspired to start your own journey that moves your offline business online to expand and accelerate growth, check out Maggie's "The Ten Deadly Mistakes When Moving Online and How to Avoid Them" here: **http://bit.ly/ten-deadly-mistakes**.

Małgorzata (Maggie) Biernacka is a Business Strategist and Effortless Transformation Coach. Her mission is to empower women to expand their offline, established businesses into the online world, bringing more impact while keeping their integrity and genuine personality.

Her professional career accelerated first in big international advertising agencies and then in corporate marketing. By the age of 35, she managed 18 markets in Europe and the Middle East, remodelling their marketing and sales strategies, always focusing on the efficiency of the activities and their positive impact on the company profit and loss. At the same time she developed her mindfulness, natural empathy, and honesty to comfortably run multinational, geographically-diverse teams.

After 25 years in the corporate world, she longed for a more balanced life and quality time with her family. The decision to drop her corporate career and start from ground zero as consultant was not easy but paid off big-time. In 2010, she received her coaching certificate and started her consulting and coaching business, supporting established business owners in their transition to an online expansion.

Maggie's Hub is a direct response to Maggie's dream and the mission to globally empower female entrepreneurs, coaches, consultants, and kick-ass experts to move their offline business online. Maggie uses her talents, expertise, and genuine personality to teach others how to fast-track their visibility and claim their expert position online. With ease. No complicated funnels needed!

Her energy level is elevated thanks to her two Vizsla dogs, which are red-haired just like Maggie! Polish by birth, she is truly an international soul.

If you would like to learn more about how Maggie can help you, she encourages you to start with the two-hour "Intensive Strategic Session." During this phenomenal, eye-opening experience you will have the opportunity to work on challenges requiring clarity and untie all the knots that hold you back. You will leave the session not only highly energized and motivated, but most importantly, with a three-stage plan that is ready to go!

To grab your Intensive Strategic Session, go to: http://bit.ly/strategic-intensive-session

CHAPTER 8

Anything is Possible

By Sharan Sammi

My way of life: Or was it?

I don't want to be a doctor!

I don't want to have an arranged marriage!

I don't want to be like everyone else and do the "right thing!"

I just want to be ME!

Growing up as a second-generation British Sikh female in the 1980's, my family followed the cultural ways of life. We did not eat meat or drink alcohol on a certain "religious day" of the week. We also did not cut our hair which was one of the attributes of following the Sikh faith. When I became a teenager, I was not allowed to go out unaccompanied or associate with boys, even as friends. We lived in a way that conformed to the Sikh community and their values of what was right and wrong, what was acceptable or could be done.

As a child, my siblings and I were expected to go to school, get an education, then maybe start working, only to get married, become a "glorified housewife" to stay at home and have children! Here we were, educated and career-minded women with the expectation from others to have no real aspirations for a thriving career! Was that what I had to look forward to? Deep down I knew there was so much to life and I did not have to settle for "living the norm." Even at this young age, I felt the pressure of what was expected, particularly from women in my cultural upbringing.

I was very quiet when I was young and often stayed "in my shell." I was a deep thinker, very intuitive, and had frequent premonitions on a normal basis. Today I realize why these feelings occurred as they were part of my psychic-medium side shining through.

In my early years, I had an ambition to be on TV as a weather presenter. My parents dismissed this idea as Indians were not on mainstream television. Did that mean I couldn't achieve my dreams of being on the TV? My parents were supportive and tried their very best to encourage me but they just wanted my siblings and me to continue our higher education which they believed would give us a solid foundation in life.

In the early stages, my parents had doubts and fears of what could be achieved in life and, HELL YES, this concern had an impact on me. At the age of 14, I joined the Duke of Edinburgh Scheme and as part of this group I had to complete a camping expedition, an overnight stay in a tent! My parents had reservations about this venture as it was overnight and also outdoors. I was determined and committed to achieve the award, so I really wanted to go. My parents supported my decision so I went and gained my bronze and silver awards, having so much fun along the way. Two years later, I made my parents proud when I achieved my Gold Award which was presented by the Duke of Edinburgh himself! We got to meet royalty at the St James Palace in London! I was also then invited as an advocate for my town to attend a lunch where I sat next to Prince Edward. The conversation was so inspiring and who would have thought I would get to socialise with royalty!

When I was eight years old, I picked up one of my Mum's magazines and found an ad for a painting competition for children. I felt an inner urge to enter as I had a strong desire to win! This feeling was my very first life experience of MANIFESTING! I used my imagination to paint a beautiful picture and entered the competition. A few weeks later, a letter came for me and I won four tickets to the local theme park. I was completely amazed and happy. This moment was the start of my journey of self-belief and self-motivation which helped me to become the serial manifestor that I am today!

Such experiences helped me realise deep down that I was put on this planet for so much MORE! I longed to stretch the boundaries and limiting beliefs which were placed upon me, to really reach for what I truly desired in life!

What Was to Evolve

After leaving University in 2002, with my Banking degree, I was faced with the positive dilemma of having three graduate banking job offers. A great position to be in but I wasn't sure which job was the right choice for my future progression. My parents fully supported my dreams at this stage in life because they just wanted to see me happy.

Making the choice between job offers was tough, but as my adrenaline pumped to the maximum, I made the strong decision to re-interview each employer! I knew I had to think outside the box! I was a little outside my comfort zone but I strongly believe, *"If you don't ask you don't get."* So, I arranged to go to each company and interview the manager.

I felt nervous and as the fear kicked in, my inner voice told me to cancel the interviews. Yet, I chose to move forward. "What can you offer me?" I confidently asked each manager of the different banks. Individually, they discussed what my position would be in more detail. I was so fascinated and as I felt in total control I pushed further. "And what about the pay? The other bank offered me this amount while you offered a smaller salary." I was afraid I had over-stepped the mark but knew I had to ask boldly.

The result: I secured the position with an Australian Bank that gave me a pay raise of 8.8% before I even started working there! My parents were surprised. They would never have dreamt of interviewing in reverse like I did. They would have settled with what was given! This moment was a strong turning point in my life when I began forming the foundations of my belief: *"If you don't ask you don't get, and if you don't try, you will never know what can be achieved!"* And yes, greatness really was achieved that day!

After completing almost a year as a Graduate in the bank, I yearned for more. Taking the inspired action, I successfully moved on to a different role within the bank. Although I deeply enjoyed the new position, I still had a yearning for more. Every time I thought about what else might be possible, I felt excited for all the unknown possibilities out there. *But it all starts with a thought, right?*

I desired change.

I desired excitement away from the 9-to-5 office position.

I desired travel, even as far away as Australia, perhaps even to relocate there.

I desired financial independence.

There was so much more to life and I wasn't living to my full potential!

Subconsciously Manifesting

I don't believe in coincidences. Circumstances happen for a reason! Once while attending a family meal, my siblings made comments about the car I drove. I was young, educated, and had a successful career but the car I drove was older than theirs. It probably seems very superficial to compare cars, but right in that moment, I put out there to the Universe my request:

"I will have a brand-new car but I will not pay for it —
I will be given it!"

Thank you

Such a powerful statement then manifested a year later. I tuned into an unfamiliar radio station to hear, "To enter the competition call…." My hands started to automatically dial the number. I got through and solved a number puzzle live on air. I then was informed that I was in a drawing with only 28 others to win a brand-new car!

On the competition day, 28 of us lined up and took part in pure-chance games involving spinning the wheel and cards. The moment was so surreal, yet magical. My heart was beating so fast and the adrenaline was pumping. And then, I WON A BRAND-NEW CAR! For the first time in my life I felt the forces of the Universe were on my side. My subconscious manifesting order from the evening with my siblings was delivered there and then! I felt joy, excitement, happiness, and a strong sensation and inner knowing that I could achieve anything in life. *Anything!* Even a NEW CAR!

In Touch with the Spirit World

The real turning point to discovering my life purpose came at the age of 25 in 2006. Work colleagues wanted to arrange a team social event, something a bit different but fun. I shared my inspired idea of attending a Psychic Medium Event in a restaurant. I had no idea what the evening would entail but I felt so deeply drawn to the advertisements; I just had to attend.

During the event, I felt tingling sensations all over my body as the medium stood up and delivered the most unbelievable spirit messages to the audience. I felt a coldness around me which I now know to be spirit presence. During this evening, I started to feel different, like an inner knowing of what needed to be said to the audience. It seemed I could also hear what the spirit was impressing upon the medium.

At the end, I enthusiastically went over to the medium and asked, "Can I have a personal reading, even if I don't know many dead people?" She laughed and said "Yes, of course! The spirit world includes your ancestors, so even those you have never known!"

The day finally arrived for my psychic-medium reading. The messages I received that day were, in fact, the starting point which changed the direction of my whole life!

The medium was given a lot of information from my Nan who is in the Spirit World and was told to tell me:

I will change where I live.

My job will be gone.

I will secure a better job position.

And the spirits are trying so hard to communicate with me – I just need to listen!

I was excited by this reading but so shocked! I felt overwhelmed and thought, "Oh fuck! That's just great. I will be homeless and, oh fuck, my job is gone too!" I never could have predicted what happened next!

The First of Many More Phone Calls to Come

Early in 2006, almost like fate in the very same week, two of my close friends phoned me and stated, "Sharan, you must attend this personal-development course held in London. You have just got to go!" I don't believe in coincidences and this opportunity was definitely not one of them.

My friend and I went down to London for an amazing, three-day, life-changing course. At the end of the first day, I did a fucking fire walk; that's how amazing it was! I actually walked on hot, burning coals! Talk about feeling the fear and doing it anyway! But what was so profound about the fire-walking experience was that all my concerns and fears just drifted away. I just decided, "Yes …I can do this fire walk."

I felt so much gratitude towards my two close friends for informing me about this course. I felt so blessed and privileged to be in the arena full of hundreds of people from around the world and to share this amazing life experience. During those few days, my whole life changed. My limiting beliefs, even those taken subconsciously from my parents, were instantly removed and healed. I totally transformed my whole belief system. I experienced this amazing feeling of empowerment that, "*Yes! Anything is possible and you really can do anything. It's all in your power, your decisions, and the choices you make in life. That's your birth-right, your freedom, it's all in your hands!*"

My life started to change.

The Second Phone Call...

In September 2006, the phone rang; a call from an old University friend. We reminisced and shared memories from our University days together. Then my friend asked if I wanted to go on holiday with her in December.

"Australia," I said and without a second thought I shouted, "For real? Okay! Let's go to AUSTRALIA!" I had this sudden rush of adrenaline and total excitement. I felt ecstatic! Once again, I was reminded there is no such thing as a coincidence. Only days earlier, I had discussed working opportunities with my manager and the possibility of a two-year secondment position with the same company in Sydney, Australia. I saw this opportunity as a gift from the Universe. So, my friend and

I booked the tickets to go to Australia over the Christmas and New Year period.

The Final Call Influencing Transformational Change in My Life

In November 2006, you guessed it, the phone rang again. This time it was from a headhunter providing details of an amazing job opportunity. Remembering my psychic reading from a few months earlier, I thought "Oh my Gosh, I have got this job in the bag. This position is already mine!"

Sitting in Starbucks, without any preparation, I waited for the interviewer to arrive. Wild thoughts ran through my head that were in total conflict. I was confused! *"What am I doing here? Do I really want a new position? Yes, I want more. NO, I am happy with my current life! Why rock the boat? Why try something new? I should just stick to what I know."*

"No!" My inner voice shouted loudly from within me, as if someone was literally behind me with a massive loudspeaker. *"Now is the time to really push yourself."* I remained nervous about what to do, but I strongly held onto that one line of psychic inspiration: *This new position is yours!*

I sat there in anticipation, the position, after all, was already granted to me! Within five minutes, the interviewer James asked, "What do you want? What will it take for you to leave the other bank and join us tomorrow in a new location?" *I would have to move, so the psychic was right about this aspect too!*

Clinging to my mug of hot chocolate, I wasn't prepared for this question. I believed I would simply be told what the salary would be. *Anything is possible though, right?* I stalled by asking multiple questions about the position, but I was internally scrambling to come up with an amount to ask for. The question came again from James, "So, Sharan, what numbers are we talking about?"

Numbers spun inside my head. I just kept hearing, "The position is yours. Even the psychic told you. This is your big break, Sharan. Let's go for more than double. It's possible, Sharan; just tell James NOW!"

I took a deep breath which helped to fill me with confidence. I spoke up loud and clear, to which James replied, "Yes!" I was so surprised, in fact in total shock. But was asking for a 120% salary increase too much? It appeared not. James said 'yes' after all! I planned to join the new bank when I returned from holiday in Australia at the beginning of the next year.

Inspiration Along the East Coast of Australia

My trip to Australia was the holiday of a lifetime. I had never travelled very far abroad, yet as tourists, we visited so many amazing places. I even got to spend a day in the Sydney office for the bank I worked for. My inner voice kept shouting "Pinch me, is this a dream?" Over those weeks, I grew very home-sick. I had never been away from my family for so long, especially during the Christmas season. I knew I would not be able to take advantage of the two-year working secondment; it was too difficult to be away from my family.

On a cruise ship travelling across the Great Barrier Reef in Australia, I sat on the open deck, feeling the sun's heat filling my whole body with a comfortable warmth while the wind blew softly. It was bliss! As I closed my eyes, I went into a deep meditative trance. Out across the ocean with a total sense of freedom, I wanted my imagination purposefully to provide inspiration and guidance on what was next for me in life. I internally asked *"If anything were possible for me, what could I accomplish?"*

"TV!" my higher mind shouted back at me.

WHAT?! My conscious mind kicked in and stirred up immediate internal conflict. "You can't appear on the TV. You have no experience and have a professional career in banking. You cannot do anything else!" Limiting beliefs on what I could achieve played out in my mind. I even recalled my childhood dream to be a weather presenter. The message truly felt surreal as I was guided towards television – my childhood dream. I felt an inner knowing that this goal was achievable.

My higher mind came through and said, "Yes, you can. ANYTHING IS POSSIBLE!"

I knew the number one rule to manifesting is to not worry about the *how*. So, I soaked up the Australian sunshine and took in the amazing fresh air while knowing deep down TV was the dream!

Conquering My Dreams

Remembering the teachings from the personal development course I attended earlier in the year, I thought about nothing else but TV. I decided to take action. I resigned from my current bank position. James held the offered position at his bank open for me to start when I was ready. But I wasn't ready just yet.

To turn my television dream into reality, I had a plan. I wrote a tailored letter to fifty individual TV acting agencies across the country. If I could convey the passion I had for acting, my confident ability, and personal drive, as well as knowledge of their agency, surely, I could get a positive response, even without any acting experience. I totally believed in this process as well as in me!

Rejection after rejection came and I grew disheartened as the days passed. I was not surprised, however, as my conscious mind kept reminding me that I had no acting experience, after all. If I didn't laugh, I would have surely cried at each rejection! I still lived in hope those next few weeks, for surely one of those fifty tailored letters would be a winner and the agency would want me.

Finally, that day arrived, the one I dreamt of. A total manifestation! I got an acceptance from an agency in the same city where I lived. I jumped for joy, amazed, in total bewilderment. Deep down felt a little like a fraud as I really didn't have any acting experience. Yet this agency was interested in me. I managed to get the courage to call the agency.

At first, I was represented on the agency's online casting pages and I started doing background work as an extra. My first assignment was for a famous UK television soap, sitting in a restaurant pretending to drink wine with others and walking into the newsagents. I quickly progressed to drama programmes and commercials with small speaking parts but I yearned for more. I guess I wanted more prestige, the hope of more fame and kudos.

I knew I was capable of so much more so I continued to press forward, continuing to put off the banking job James held for me. I knew that if I didn't try now, I would never know if TV was really for me. I would never find out what I was really capable of and I didn't want to regret my decisions.

I discussed my desires with my agent. "I am unique," I told him. "I am confident and have so much motivation and inner drive. I am capable of better roles; just give me the opportunity and I will prove it."

I continued to face 'no' after 'no,' for what felt like a year. Finally, I got the call, the one I wished for. My agent offered me the opportunity to attend a casting for a part in a major TV Soap. I jumped at the chance.

During the audition, fear ran through me as I looked around the room at the other candidates. My nerves kicked in. "What are you doing here, Sharan?" my conscious mind screamed at me. "RUN!" I took a deep breath and affirmed to myself "I can do this – anything is possible and this is possible for me right now." I began to act as if I had already been given the part. My confidence grew by the second, so I smiled and completed the audition.

The Dream Phone Call

The call came that evening. My dream came true and changed the course of my life, yet again! I got the part. I just couldn't believe it! Me, YES me: that inexperienced TV-star wannabe! I got the part for real!

Working on the television Soap alongside the famous cast was mind-blowing. To think that I, a professional with a banking degree, totally changed direction and conquered unchartered territory – with no acting experience. This event felt amazing and deepened my belief that Anything is Possible.

In front of the camera, I loved the whole kudos. My part felt so powerful, exciting, and important to the storylines. This experience was what I longed for as a child, to act on TV and find fame in front of the camera.

A month passed and I was offered a permanent role. Yet, I didn't feel the excitement I thought I would. The role required very early mornings, long working days, and a lot of waiting around on set. I had no say on the clothes, hair, or makeup; I just learned my words. I felt bored, even deflated. I thought acting on TV would be more exciting. I was disappointed and felt totally unfulfilled. I didn't feel I was using my true ability and potential, namely my brain power. I felt a strong urge back towards the banking world that would give me the personal drive and satisfaction to use my mathematical brain!

Following My Passion

I ended the TV contract and signed the bank contract with James. But before I did, I secured more tangible benefits and even an increase in pay. *If you don't ask – you don't get!* A few years later, I got married to my soulmate, had two amazing earth angels, and moved into our six-bedroom showroom home. I went on to launch a successful, empowering coaching business that has touched the lives of over 5,000 women from around the globe and is growing on a daily basis.

My business is based on the foundations of Living your Dream Life where Anything is Possible. I help put solid foundations in place for you through my coaching programs to help you take inspired action, turning your dreams into reality and living your life on your terms. So, whether you ultimately need to work on confidence or self-esteem issues or even removing fears and limiting beliefs, I can help you work through these concerns in a safe environment that allows you to grow and develop.

So, if you desire incredible, life-changing results in any area of your life, from changing careers, financial abundance, relationships and attracting your most compatible soulmate, to overcoming stresses, trauma, and illnesses, reach out today. You will benefit on all levels including emotional, mental, physical, financial, and spiritual. Living life on your own terms is an amazing feeling!

So How Does Your Dream Life Look?

Let's take the impossible, spin it across the Universe, and open up the vibrational forces to endless possibilities. The power is within you!

Throughout my journey, living my life on my own terms gave me an amazing sense of personal power. I discovered the true meaning of life and what was and still is possible for me. From doing a fire walk, to manifesting a brand-new car, from turning down a secondment opportunity in Australia, to working as a TV actress – anything is possible!

You must open up your imagination and really go deep, asking yourself, "What is it that I desire? What are my ultimate dreams, aspirations, and goals?" The answers to those questions are the foundations for your action plan, to really manifest the life you truly deserve. Yes, fears and inner conflicts will come through but manifesting requires you to conquer these doubts and turn that energy into a strong sense of self-belief, determination, and inner drive. This action will enable you to live the life of your dreams. If you want something in life, reach out and accomplish greatness!

One of my fundamental core beliefs and a deep-rooted value is:

Nothing is Impossible, Anything is Possible, and you can do anything if you put your mind, body, soul, spirit, and heart into it!

I did it... SO CAN YOU!

Come and join my tribe where YES…Anything is Possible!

https://www.facebook.com/groups/AnythingisPossibleFor You/

Sharan is an inspirer and motivator with the sole aim of shining light everywhere she goes. As an empowerment life coach, NLP (Neuro-Linguistic Programming) Master Practitioner, and Theta Healing Practitioner, Sharan aims to heal limiting beliefs held deep in the subconscious and transform the lives of her soul clients.

On another spectrum, Sharan was also a professional in the UK Corporate Banking World. She really does appreciate that everything is *simply energy!* As part of her life's mission, Sharan is actively working on bringing the two worlds together by integrating powerful holistic methodology to the corporate hemisphere.

As part of her life purpose, Sharan works with women around the globe, helping to influence major breakthroughs against life's challenges. Sharan appreciates that each woman is unique, but in most cases, deep-rooted fears, doubts, concerns, and lack of confidence stop individuals from excelling in life.

Sharan helps women reach their true potential in all areas of life by teaching empowerment strategies to gain confidence, self-esteem, and control over their own lives. Examples range from gaining prestigious employment positions, dramatically increasing earning, taking the courage to resign from the "job" and become self-employed, to meeting soulmates and forming amazing relationships.

With the belief that *"Anything is Possible"* Sharan really does empower her clients to embrace the life of their ultimate dreams. So, no bullshit or excuses will stand in the way! Her mission is to inspire her soul clients to harness the power of self-belief.

From qualifying as a hairdresser at 18, achieving two University degrees, winning a brand-new car, holidays, and money, to landing a role on a popular UK TV soap without any prior acting experience, Sharan truly lives by the principal "Life is what you make it!" She is now married to her soulmate and has two adorable earth angels.

Come and join Sharan in her Facebook group, *Anything is Possible*, where she offers daily inspiration, motivation, and much more.

https://www.facebook.com/groups/AnythingisPossibleFor You/

Contact Sharan directly through her website www.blessence.co.uk and if you quote *Wild Wise Women*, you will receive 15% off all individual sessions, including reading, healings, and one-to-one coaching sessions.

Live the Life of your Dreams where Anything is Possible!

CHAPTER 9:

Create Pure Joy in Your Life

By Daria Ates

It's February 2012, another dark, cold, and rainy day. I lay on the bed wondering, "Is it the weather that makes me feel this awful?" I barely have enough energy to get myself up from the bed to get a glass of water or to use the bathroom! My hair keeps falling out. I put weight on even though I can't be bothered to eat; sleeping is the only activity I feel like I can manage. My memory is so bad that it terrifies me. My skin is dry and it cracks painfully. My scalp is so itchy it makes me scratch until it bleeds! Finally, I realise my problems can't be caused just by the weather. These symptoms have lasted for several months.

I book an appointment to run a blood test. A few days later my doctor tells me the blood test results reveal that I have Hashimoto's disease. It. Is. A. Lifetime. Disease. They can do nothing but keep my symptoms under control with medication for the rest of my life. Full stop.

Leaving the building, I burst into tears. The word INCURABLE keeps popping up in my mind like a flashing red sign. I decide to find some research and see what I can do for myself to feel better.

After a several hours of study and research on the disease, information about both conventional and not-so-conventional treatment, I realise to find the right answers to all my questions is not going to be as easy as I thought. There is so much information out there; going through it all is extremely time-consuming and absolutely exhausting. Deciding what is truly helpful feels difficult and overwhelming. Am I really capable to see this through? Why do I still feel miserable, even after several months of taking the drugs that are supposed to keep my symptoms "under control?" I would almost rather take a massive overdose to escape from this horrible suffering!

Then I realise there are people out there who suffer much more than I do and make the decision to reach out for help. I find an alternative medicine doctor who recommends natural medication replacement. Then I start visiting a holistic doctor and acupuncturist, a brilliant human being and teacher. His calm energy makes me feel safe. He teaches me that all my health issues most likely started 20 years previously, when I was involved in an almost-fatal car crash.

I spent seven months in the hospital, where I received massive amounts of antibiotics into my system to fight possible infections. I was a mum of two young children, but I couldn't see them for the seven months, the first time I was ever away from them since they were born. They weren't allowed into the Trauma Unit where I was admitted. I even missed my son's first day at school! I missed them to bits, and cried secretly at nights. After being finally discharged from the hospital, I spent another three years as an outpatient, coming back for a physio therapy on weekly basis to learn to walk again.

Now I know that this incident was the very first trigger for my immune system to turn against me. The holistic doctor says all that stress has an enormous impact on my body and health, even though it took many, many years for first symptoms to start appearing.

I begin to grow stronger physically and emotionally while visiting him for about two years, however, I still don't feel my usual self. I know there is still something missing. I feel strong enough to start working but there is only a certain number of hours and activities I can manage to focus on before I get exhausted again. My hair stops falling and there is even remarkable weight loss due to following some diet changes I find helpful for Hashimoto's patients. My brain fog, however, is still a big concern for me.

I then learn about Intermittent Fasting, where you allow your body to heal by choosing two days a week without food at all, providing it with freshly squeezed juices to supply all the necessary nutrients. The truth is, the body can either digest or heal, but not both at the same time. Following a special protocol, I learn how to repair my intestines, damaged from loads of chemicals from stress, processed food, water, and environmental factors. Particles from these negative sources then entered into the blood stream through my damaged intestinal walls. These particles cause the inflammation in the body and even slight food allergies. If this issue is not addressed for a long period of time, then various symptoms start occurring, like food allergies, tiredness and lack of concentration, loss of motivation, or weight gain.

For me, it makes sense to avoid gluten totally as I start to heal, since Hashimoto's causes my immune system to mistake the cells of my thyroid gland with the gluten cells that are not supposed to be present in the blood stream. My immune system then attacks my thyroid gland which causes a myriad of symptoms.

After several months of intermittent fasting, I make an appointment for a follow-up blood test with my regular General Practitioner. The results are good and the doctor is pleased. But when I share with her about the changes I implemented into my life, she frowns, turns her head and for the first time, properly looks at me over her huge glasses. "Your medication works; the results have nothing to do with gluten." Little did she know, her medication was resting deep in my drawer, waiting for its better days!

And then one day, devastating news presents itself. My brother, a father of two young children, not even 40 years old himself, took his own life. That information is a massive shock for my already compromised immune system. My symptoms start creeping back while new ones start appearing, even though I still keep following my holistic doctor's advice about chemicals. No matter how I can control my physical and environmental stress, I cannot control, at least at this time and in this situation, my emotional stress response. Once again, I am exhausted most of the time, I cannot focus on anything, and I cry all the time. My scalp starts feeling itchy and sore again. And then one day, I even find out there is a bald patch at the back of my head! I am terrified. How can I carry on with all these issues? Am I going to end up without any hair whatsoever? I know I need to do something, but I just cannot think clearly at all.

Forcing myself into another round of study and research to find out how to clear my mind from constant worrying and anxiety that leads to depression, I stubbornly dig into anything and everything I can possibly think of. I find out there is another prevalent cause of many autoimmune diseases, such as Hashimoto's, as well as the majority of fatal health issues, like heart attacks, strokes, or even cancer. It is present in our day-to-day life, the so-called silent killer -- STRESS. Due to my constant brain fog I forgot entirely that my holistic doctor told me exactly that fact. There are three different types of stress: physical, emotional, and environmental. They all show up in various ways and create different chemicals in our body and brain that are toxic to us.

At last, I realise I have to address each type of stress in my life in order to eliminate its negative impact. I learn how to meditate, slowly at first, just for five to ten minutes to observe my breath and be present. This practice helps to calm my mind and decreases both physical and emotional stress. Then, I work on how to replace all the cleaning materials and skincare products in my household with clean alternatives. I even start making my own toothpaste, body lotion, and antiperspirant to make sure they are clear of chemicals. This practice addresses any environmental stress, as most cleaning and even personal-care products are loaded with toxic chemicals that are harmful to our health.

Once I make these changes, I can feel my memory start improving, I become more energetic and motivated to beat this monster called autoimmune disorder. I slowly begin to include light exercise into my routine to strengthen my immune system. First, I take short, brisk walks, to increase my heart rate. Then I try different activities like Pilates or hiking.

Finally, I fall in love with Yoga and Qi Gong, which is a combination of martial arts and energy work.

I spend thousands of pounds on different personal development programs to learn how to meditate in a correct and useful way for me and how to change my mind-set and perception. But the most helpful technique I discover is Tapping, the popular name for EFT (Emotional Freedom Techniques). Tapping is one of many modalities of Energy work, a kind of Energy Psychology. After seeing many people's outstanding results, I try it for myself and the practice resonates with me enormously.

Out of curiosity I decide to find a local practitioner to see if Tapping is a process that can help me with my healing. After just one therapy session I feel as if a huge weight is lifted from my shoulders and I find myself singing along the sidewalk on my way home! After all those years of worry, anxiety, and depression from both physical and emotional pain, I suddenly feel all the possibilities in life open for me. I can achieve anything! I decide to learn more about this technique, because if it can work so beautifully for me, I want to learn how to help others to see there IS help and hope!

After finding a master trainer and a mentor, I start diving into the magic of Energy Psychology work and I love it. It takes time to learn an art and develop the skills needed, but learning this type of work is the most adventurous journey I could have ever imagined. I learn, for example, that highly-sensitive people are born with larger amygdala, a roughly almond-sized mass of grey matter inside our brain, involved with experiencing emotions. This issue happens when some kind of trauma happens even before they are born. That information resonates with me, a highly-sensitive person, because I know what my Mother went through while pregnant with me, including being betrayed and abandoned by my father.

During the training and practicing one of the modalities, I experience an extraordinary revelation that helps put all the bits and pieces together for me. I finally am able to understand and forgive my Mother for her lack of love for me and rejection I felt for most of my adult life. Sadly, she passed away a few months prior to my enlightening experience. But forgiving her allows me to heal many past hurts.

I start working with clients in my clinic and due to my highly-developed intuition, they experience marvellous results. For instance, one client had a backache that caused her to suffer for over three weeks. No painkiller suggested by her doctor helped at all, but her pain diminished within 20 minutes of working with me. She bounces around, thanking me, smiling, and asking what woo-doo this is!

Another client came to me for his anxiety, depression, and panic attacks even after attending conventional talking therapy and being on medication for seven years. He was worried since he started noticing suicidal thoughts. He dreaded going out with his friends, let alone starting a relationship with a woman, after a previous experience broke his heart. About eight weeks after the end of our therapy sessions, he is able to use the tools he was equipped with when he feels he needs a bit of support. So, he sent me this message:

Hi Daria. Just texting you to let you know that I've been doing great since our last meet. I've been out and about loads more and I've actually been seeing someone which has been a big step forward for me too. No chance I could have done this a few months ago. You've been such a big help and I just want to thank you again for it all…

After some time working with clients with all sorts of physical, emotional, and mental health issues, I came to the realisation that my own autoimmune symptoms are getting better too. The more I work and Tap with clients, the better I feel myself. I came to realise that clearing all sorts of unresolved issues from our pasts, hidden in our subconscious minds, actually helps with autoimmune symptoms too!

Despite what others say, there IS a hope. That awareness is a huge revelation and relief to me. I actually feel more energetic, less stressed and overwhelmed, and I enjoy my life much more. This realisation is the basis for creating a programme for people like me, who have their businesses, yet struggle with a lack of energy, brain fog, and physical and emotional pain that stop them from building their empire and achieving their desires in a big way.

Now I won't lie; in the beginning of my healing process, it wasn't always easy to follow my findings, such as the very strict diet or time management. I still get overwhelmed at times as I am a work in progress. I am a human and at the end of the day, life is a process. Some days I feel marvellous but other days I can feel challenged by daily tasks. But now I have tools I can use when I feel that I need a bit more support to get my energy level back on track. And I love helping others achieve the same.

Every day I make a choice to look for opportunities to be grateful. Every day I decide to look for occasions to be pleasantly surprised. Every day I look for the good. I am grateful for the pain I once felt because it made me stronger and wiser. I am grateful for the pain I will feel in the future because it will bring me closer to my dreams.

Now I have various tools to support my physical, emotional, and spiritual well-being when I need it. It took eight years of research, study and training, lots of pain, trials and errors, as well as thousands of pounds to get where I am today. I now use this knowledge, art, and skill to help entrepreneurs and business owners to achieve their desires without having to go through all those trials. I don't want anyone else to lose their hope and feel as helpless as I once did. Now I am equipped with knowledge, techniques, experiences, and passion to create a solution that guides my clients through their own transformation from overwhelmed, tired, and unfulfilled entrepreneurs into Creators of Pure Joy in Their Lives. We use techniques such as Deep State RePattering, the Movie Technique, Inner-Child Therapy, Mindfulness-Based Inner RePattering, Tearless Trauma, and the Chase-the-Pain Technique.

I am endlessly grateful for my clients' successes and ability to grow and build their businesses and lives almost effortlessly, without having to push through until they fall off the track.

They say time heals. Time is not quite enough.
Often it needs more support.

If you feel ready to unleash yourself from your limiting beliefs that hold you back from who you truly are and set yourself up for exponential growth of both your business and personal life, click here to get Daria's FREE 20-minute video session, "Experience Peace Through Colourful Breathing (worth £497) at www.dariascoaching.com.

Daria Ates is a Physical, Emotional, and Spiritual Energy Coach who offers a unique/bespoke solution to mind, body, and soul healing. After many years of trials and errors on her own journey to heal from two so-called incurable autoimmune diseases, she now works with entrepreneurs and change makers who often feel tired, overwhelmed, and stressed while trying to balance both their businesses and personal lives, often causing a negative impact on their health. She leads them step-by-step to their desired physical, emotional, and spiritual joy and overall wellbeing so they can create abundance, not only in their businesses, but in all areas of their lives.

Daria is a great believer in energy work and quantum field. She is on mission to impact millions via her work to prevent her clients from suffering the way she had to on her own lonely healing journey. She now helps successful entrepreneurs and influencers from all over the world learn how to reverse their symptoms and find the energy they crave.

Daria is fun to be around and loves spending time travelling the world with her young grandchildren, singing lullabies for them and reading tales before bed across the continents.

If you feel ready to unleash yourself from your limiting beliefs that hold you back from who you truly are and set yourself up for exponential growth of both your business and personal life, click here to get Daria's FREE "Tap into Unlimited Abundance Blueprint", a two-week training course at www.dariascoaching.com

CHAPTER 10

The Least Likely Leader

By Magdalena Gabriah

I was having a quiet cup of coffee in my beautiful home situated in a quiet residential area surrounded by good schools. The sense of peace was overwhelming. I could not remember ever feeling this much at peace. My two-year-old baby was soundly asleep upstairs and I went back in my mind to the place where it all started.

I arrived in London on a cold January day in 2003, to live as an au-pair with a family of five and to start a new chapter in my life. I had £50.00 and a suitcase with me; that was the sum of all my belongings, all I had.

The first six months of living in the UK were pure bliss; there was not a day when I did not think how lucky I was. However, as time progressed, the reality of living with someone else's family started to hit home; first it was the fact that I was never allowed to invite friends over, then I noticed that my hours of work started to increase. Soon, I was working almost around the clock, including weekends and bank holidays for less than the minimum wage. The niggling feeling of being trapped by my circumstances started to dawn on me and I realised that if I didn't change the direction my life was heading, then I was going to be a live-in housekeeper for the rest of my life!

This picture was not the future I dreamed of. Yearning for a family of my own and a place I could call home, I realised that if I wanted my life to change, then I would have to change myself first. But where should I even start?

Before arriving in the UK, I had finished Music School in my native Poland. Although I always enjoyed music, dancing, and singing, school was not an easy place for me. I was a shy and a self-contained person. I found it difficult to build relationships with others and it took me a very long time to turn acquaintances into friendships. I felt like I did not belong and that somehow that I was inferior to those around me. My grandma said that I was a very thoughtful child. I wish I had known back then that I had what I now know to be early signs of introversion.

Another reason why I struggled at the music school was that I was not really cut out for public appearances. Before each performance, my heart started pounding in my chest, my hands got sweaty, and I even convinced myself that I had forgotten parts of the piece which inevitably resulted in mistakes. I felt doomed for failure.

I did not realise that all these symptoms led up to one result - - performance anxiety. Unfortunately, nobody at my school ever talked about performance anxiety or prepared us to manage it, so I assumed that my inability to perform perfectly in public was another one of my failings. The anxiety made me even more insecure and introverted amongst my peers and teachers.

I had to endure all these battles on my own as I did not have a lot of support at home. My dad was a very hard and a difficult man to please. There was nothing short of almost perfection that I could do to keep him happy. And when we failed, he used his position of power to show my sister and me what he thought of us. Sometimes he pulled our ears or banged our heads together; he told us we were "stupid" or "ignorant," and ordered us to do dozens of sit-ups. When we were most unlucky, he took his leather belt and struck us repeatedly.

My mum did her best to shield us, but even she failed when faced with his overbearing power. She also found herself on the receiving end of his wrath, our house filled with music... and arguments. After years of falling out and trying to make amends with each other my parents finally split up when I was 18 years old.

The introversion, performance anxiety, and problems at home started to affect I how saw myself, my abilities, and my future. Not only did I lose my confidence and self-assurance; I also lost any sense of feeling safe and secure. Being in a loving relationship became an impossible dream, but something within me refused to give up on that dream just yet.

The opportunity to come to England as an au-pair gave me a glimmer of hope and a fresh start. I had a shot at creating the life I always wanted, even if I did not exactly know how the future would unfold.

When I arrived in England, I was driven, I was relentless; I was not going to let go of my chance to have a fresh start. Failure was not even in my vocabulary. I knew that I could not go back to Poland -- my mum had moved to the U.S. and my sister to Italy. Sadly, there was no longer a home for me to return to. So, for the next 16 years, I worked very, very hard, starting at the bottom of the career ladder working as an au pair.

Eighteen months after I arrived in the UK, I realised that being an au pair for life was not going to work; I craved to have a family and a home of my own. I wanted to feel safe and to feel loved. That is when I knew, I had to start thinking strategically about my goals, dreams, and aspirations. I had to plan how I would go about achieving them. The beginnings were difficult; I just did not know what direction to take, but I started to see progress when I focussed on removing stumbling blocks one at a time. Looking back on those days, I realise that I was taking my first steps to coaching myself, even if I did not recognize what I was doing at the time.

There was a lot that I had to learn over those years. There were plenty of failures and disappointments I had to endure, but I have no regrets about staring on this journey. Every step I took, whether right or wrong, brought me closer to where I am now, sharing my story with others. Along the way, there were turning points that gave me continuing hope for the future.

The first point came after I entered university to study music. Certainly, I did not even have the slightest audacity to dream of going to University when I first arrived in the UK. But circumstances just miraculously aligned and I arrived at Brunel University for a three-year bachelor's degree course in music.

After escaping my housekeeping career, the ability to surround myself with creative, thought-provoking people felt very liberating. Studying music gave me an opportunity to change the direction of my life and feel almost at home with what I was once was familiar with. At the start, I seemed to have forgotten my performance anxiety from almost ten years before. However, the old feelings of pressure reappeared and I had to face the music, literally!

I soon realised that, although my performance anxiety had not gone away altogether, I was able to cope with it better. Perhaps the experience of forging a new life for myself in a foreign country gave me the confidence I once lacked. Perhaps it was the perspective of time that helped me see that the worries I once had were now committed to the past. I do, however, give the most credit in making the situation better to the university tutors. They embraced all of us students and seemed focussed on nourishing and supporting our musicianship, instead of highlighting our flaws and shortcomings. It was also at Brunel University where I heard about performance anxiety for the very first time in my life and understood how big the problem really was as I began to research further. I chose to make this subject the focus of my dissertation.

Discovering that the anxiety that crippled me for so many years was a phenomenon that 47% of performers suffer from was a massive turning point for me. I also discovered tools and techniques that are helpful when managing anxiety. For the first time in a long while I did not feel like a failure, like someone who lacked basic skills and confidence -- someone who was different from the norm. Instead I felt normal, accepted, and that I belonged. The university gave me a second chance in life. A beam of hope began to reach me through the clouds that shrouded my past, and I started dreaming of a brighter future, believing that it was truly possible.

The second turning point that completely changed my life came years later. I had successfully pursued a corporate career for a number of years. Then, as part of personal development as a prospective future leader within the company, I was offered a personality questionnaire. It was called a Personal Impact Report and was prepared using the Myers-Briggs Type Indicator (MBTI). To start with I had no idea what the MBTI was, but I was told that if I completed a set of questions, the report would help to establish what my personality type was and how it could affect my leadership style.

When my coach explained the results of the findings, she said the report showed that I might have a preference for introversion. She asked if I knew what that word meant. I said, "Yes," but I really had no clue. She explained to me the observable behaviours in people who have a preference for introversion include:

- A need to think things through before communicating them out loud
- A need to spend time on quiet reflection to understand things around them or events that have taken place.
- A need to take time out after interactions with people to re-charge.
- The preference for maintaining deeper friendships instead of having a wide circle of friends.

My coach also explained that introversion and extroversion in the MBTI context are considered to be equally valuable; they just have different strengths and development areas. She said that from the MBTI perspective and its ethos, being extroverted was equally as good as being introverted.

I will never forget that day. I sat at my desk and the realisation struck me that this test revealed who I was: I was an introvert and that was okay! The implications of having a preference for introversion and not extraversion meant that I saw the world differently and that I interacted with it in a unique way. I now knew *why* all these years, since the time I was a child, I found it difficult to build new relationships, and why once I was comfortable with someone, I created long-lasting connections. My approach to the world did not mean that I lacked something, it just meant that I was different.

I felt a huge sense of relief that day, and freedom that comes from knowing who I was and finally accepting who I was for the first time in my life.

I was 32-years old then!

I don't generally believe in having regrets in life, but if only I had a chance to understand my true self sooner, I could have avoided the self-limiting beliefs I adopted along the way. I said "no," to so many opportunities, believing I would not be able to see them through.

This realisation of who I truly am is why in 2018, I left my corporate role and since then I have spent my time developing a number of coaching programmes based on what I learnt during my journey, either from music, psychology, or neuroscience. I share how I overcame my own challenges and the methodologies I utilise when inspiring, empowering, and motivating others. I am a founder and owner of the coaching, training, and a personal-development company called Forte Training Company. The word "forte" is often used to describe someone's strength or an area of expertise. For me, Forte means recognizing that our weaknesses can be turned into strengths, if we accept the opportunity to explore and understand them better. The areas that we might perceive as our weaknesses are actually the gifts that make us unique. With the right support, these areas can be turned into our greatest strengths and assets.

At Forte, we also believe that inspired people inspire, and empowered people empower which is why we not only help our clients discover their potential, we also prepare them to pay their way forward by supporting and building others up. We are passionate about creating a network of people who, once their own lives and careers have been transformed, want to make a positive difference in the world.

And what about music? Performance coaching is still not widely accessible for musicians, which is why my husband and I set up Ascot Music School. There we not only teach our students how to play an instrument but also how to win the mind-battle of performance anxiety. We incorporate coaching and performance master classes in our curriculum for each student.

Knowing that I can pass the lessons I learnt about the transformational power of coaching and personal development to the next generation brings me great pleasure and satisfaction. I feel like my journey did not occur in vain. All the years when my life was far from picture-perfect were simply the preparation for me to share my story with others. As a result of these lessons, I want to illustrate the point that there is hope, that we can turn our lives around and make them beautiful. We also have an opportunity to make our journeys worthwhile. Coaching and developing people are my ways of paying forward my gratitude for where this journey has brought me, as well as for the support and encouragement I received along the way.

I look again around my peaceful home and realise how much my life has changed since I arrived in the UK with a £50 note and a suitcase. I have been blessed with this beautiful place I call home and a loving family of my own. But perhaps the biggest change happened invisibly, inside of me, in how I see myself. And maybe this view is all the evidence we need to believe in our own strengths, our own unique set of supcrpowers. If only we would believe....

As a classically trained pianist, Magdalena Gabriah has the innate ability to hone senses and skills through the art of music and psychology of performance. Having obtained both a degree in music and multiple coaching qualifications, Magdalena has a set of unique skills, real-life experience, and a refreshing perspective on people and performance.

Magdalena was nominated in 2019, and became the finalist of two categories: Female Entrepreneur of the Year and Start Up of the Year for her Forte Training Company.

However, success was not always easy for Magdalena; her love for music once was a shield for the challenges she faced in her life whilst trying to fit in and failing as she viewed the world through the lens of introversion and performance anxiety. The combination of these factors pulled her back from fully embracing life, not realising she had the ability to dissolve the invisible walls by appreciating her unique combination of values, purpose, and personality.

Through working on her own situation, Magdalena gained an empathic focus and understanding of why many people struggle to live the lives they envision for themselves. By applying her own learning and deploying the latest scientific developments, she supports others to lead the lives they have always yearned to have.

Magdalena is the founder of Forte Training Company and co-founder of Ascot Music School where she gives back by empowering others to reach their full potential, then pay it forward by being the force for good. Her message is one of empowerment. *Do not believe those who have ever said that you alone are powerless. Whatever you are aspiring for, I know you have everything you need to make your own mark on the world, to be the driving force of positive change, that like a note committed to a room full of people has no other option than to ring out its pure brilliance."*

If you are interested in starting a journey of personal transformation or would like to join a community that inspires, empowers, and motivates leaders, contact Magdalena and her team at https://www.fortetrainingcompany.com to discuss how they can support you.

Work With Me

At an all-time low I considered shutting all my business ventures down. I kept spinning my wheels while getting nowhere, desperately trying to move the needle in my business. Yet, my coaching business still wasn't where I wanted it to be...

I spent hours upon hours on social media with very little to no return. I was at the end of my rope, ready to just pack up and leave.

This feeling of defeat occurred just a few short months before I successfully launched and published my bestselling book.

I have completely transformed my business and life since publishing my first book and went from working 15-hour days, trying every single business strategy out there and pulling my hair out of desperation, to claiming a fully-booked status.

Here are some of the accomplishments I have achieved since publishing my first book:

- I was featured as a guest expert on two podcasts within a week (without me having to lift a finger) as a direct result of having my book published and got three clients out of it

- A prominent blogger reached out to interview me and featured my story that same week

- I was offered the opportunity to place my books on bedsides in five-star hotels, such as the Waldorf Astoria (they have a very stringent approval process) and to appear in the media

- The Females Entrepreneurs Network sought me out to feature my story

- I was offered a traditional publishing deal that I have since turned down. As a self-published author, I am empowered enough to know I am the prize, not the publishing house

- I was approved as the leader of WomanSpeak, a company that offers the most innovative, effective training for women speakers and leaders in the world and effectively catapulted my public-speaking career in the process

- I was invited to speak at a women's conference in London and received another opportunity to be a guest speaker at women's empowerment event soon after

- I have tripled my rates and my income more than doubled; my business keeps going from strength to strength

Still not convinced?

Sister, I have walked in your shoes.

I know what's it's like to keep spinning your wheels and get nowhere, wondering where the next payment will come from.

Let me tell you, working 15-hour days is not a sustainable way to grow a heart-centred business. I know. I tried.

But I also know what it's like to wake up to new subscribers, booked discovery calls, and email payment notifications.

If I, a girl from a post-communist country with broken English can do it, what's stopping you?

But don't just take my word for it. Book a **FREE 20-Minute "Get Your Book Done In 90 Days" Assessment** now to validate your book or book idea. Write and publish your book now so you can finally have the breakthrough you waited for all those lean years!

Get those little fingers clicking and claim your spot here before it's too late:

https://leapafraid.com/wise

Psst! You'll be glad you did!

No Time to Write a Book?

Get Published the Easy Way and Co-Author
a Bestselling Book Instead

**Do you secretly dream of one day becoming a
published bestselling author but don't have the time or
the energy to put your own book out there?**

What if you could get all the perks of being a published
bestselling author without spending hours upon hours doing
the research, learning how keywords work, or perfecting the
manuscript?

What if you could fast-track your path to bestselling author
status, exponentially catapult your coaching or healing
business and finally have the breakthrough you've been
waiting for all those lean years?

Imagine, landing speaking gigs, being interviewed as an expert,
getting fully booked with soul, high-end clients, doubling or
tripling your rates, and being the sought-out expert in your
niche.

Sister, look no further because co-authoring a bestselling book
is the answer to your prayers! Throw overwhelm out the
window, co-authoring a bestselling book is the easiest way to
live life.

All you have to do to participate in the next anthology is to
turn in your story in just like all the women in this book did
and let me take care of the rest. That's my promise to you!

I'll show you the exact steps you need to take to speak to the hearts and souls of your ideal clients so you can make the biggest impact, income, and influence with your story. Forget about the technical gremlins; I eat them for breakfast! I'll have the book published for you, thus guaranteeing the bestseller status. Plus, I'm even going to have your story expertly edited by my dazzling team.

Go here for details on the next project:
https://leapafraid.com/anthology/

Can You Help?

Thank You for Reading *Wild Wise Women*!

We poured all our hearts, souls, malbec, amaretto, Baileys, Jack Daniels, tea with rum and a dash of honey, maca, yerba mate, ginger kombucha, double espresso, green smoothies, and an extra-large chai into this book. (Editor's note: No husbands were harmed in the making of this book.)

We really value your feedback and would appreciate if you could leave an honest review and share your biggest takeaways and aha-moments. We promise we will read every comment as we care about YOU more than we care about our beverage supplies.

We need your input to replenish our beverages supply to make the next version of this book and our future books better (Hey, a girl needs a drink to get her creative juices flowing!)

If you got this far, the chances are you enjoyed our book unless, of course, it's the magic of the coffee beans or tea leaves that helped you make it through. (Yawn!)

Either way, please leave us an honest review on Amazon and let us know what you thought of the book!

Thanks a million,
Wild Wise Women xx

Printed in Poland
by Amazon Fulfillment
Poland Sp. z o.o., Wrocław

54478013R00090